EVERY SALAD EVER

EVERY SALAD EVER

From Grains to Greens
and Pasta to Beans
plus Every Salad in Betweens

GRETA PODLESKI

CLARKSON POTTER / PUBLISHERS
New York

Clarkson Potter/Publishers
An imprint of the Crown Publishing Group
A division of Penguin Random House LLC
1745 Broadway
New York, NY 10019
clarksonpotter.com
penguinrandomhouse.com

Orignally self-published in Canada by the author in 2025.

Library of Congress Cataloging-in-Publication Data is available upon request.

ISBN 979-8-217-03679-0
Ebook ISBN 979-8-217-03680-6

Edited by Fina Scroppo
Book Design by REES + STAGER Inc.
Food Photography and Styling by Greta Podleski

Author Photos
Hilary Gauld (back cover, pages 204, 285, 288, inside back cover)
Leigh Sellner Photography (pages 2, 52, 70–71, 166, 184–185, 286)
Nicole Gingrich, REES + STAGER Inc. (pages 6, 8, 11, 13, 14, 32–33, 92, 110–111, 128, 148–149, 222–223, 246, 272, 274)

Manufactured in China

10 9 8 7 6 5 4 3 2 1

First US Edition

The authorized representative in the EU for product safety and compliance is Penguin Random House Ireland, Morrison Chambers, 32 Nassau Street, Dublin D02 YH68, Ireland, https://eu-contact.penguin.ie.

Recipe analysis calculated using Nutritionist Pro™ software (www.nutritionistpro.com). When a choice of ingredients is listed, analysis is calculated using the first ingredient. Optional ingredients are not included in the analysis.

DEDICATION

To King Rico,

His Majesty, The Pilferer of Parmesan,
The Sovereign of Stolen Croutons,
His Royal Highness of Bootlegged Bacon,
The Monarch of Missing Morsels
and The Ruler of My Heart...

This one's for you, my fur-ever friend.
Please don't eat the pages.

CONTENTS

Introduction
9

Grainy Goodness
Hop on the grain train! Next stop, salad heaven.
15

Greens Galore
Fresh and flavorful leafy legends.
53

Pasta Palooza
Oodles of noodle salads.
93

The Bean Scene
Beautiful, bountiful salads featuring chickpeas, beans and lentils.
129

The Classics
If it ain't broke, don't fix it!
167

The In-Betweens
These outstanding outliers are in a category all by themselves. Literally.
205

The Embellishments
Edible exclamation points, salad toppers and protein boosters.
247

Acknowledgments
273

Index
275

Metric Conversions
287

INTRODUCTION

I had a dream.

I was seated in the studio audience watching the taping of an episode of *Friends*. Monica was standing in her funky apartment kitchen, whipping up a recipe from *Every Salad Ever*.

Chandler, seated at the table, picked up my cookbook and thumbed through it with exaggerated flair. "Could there BE any more salads in here?" He slammed the book shut with mock drama just as Joey walked in.

"Hey, Mon, what's for dinner?" Joey asked, sniffing the air like a hound on the scent. Without missing a beat, Chandler replied, "Take a wild guess. It starts with 'sal' and ends with 'ad.'" Joey frowned. "Salad? Salads are for sissies! I like MAN FOOD!" He pounded his chest with his fist like Tarzan.

Monica rolled her eyes and handed Joey a heaping bowl of my Loaded Italian Pasta Salad. "Well, you're in luck, Joey. This one's got pasta, salami and cheese—basically your three food groups."

Joey stared at the salad, his eyes wide with delight. Cradling the bowl like a long-lost love, he delivered his classic line in his trademark flirty tone, "How YOU doin'?"

The audience roared with laughter, and I woke up with a smile, thinking, *If it's good enough for Joey Tribbiani, it's good enough for the world!*

I'm obsessed with *Friends*, and I'm equally obsessed with salads.

Back in the '70s, when Mom made salad for me and my five sisters, we knew exactly what we were getting: iceberg lettuce, a few token tomato wedges (Did grape tomatoes even exist?) and some grated carrots for color. That was the holy trinity of homemade salads—there were no frills, no surprises and certainly no arugula.

As for dressing? We had three choices: bottled Ranch, French or Thousand Island. I've never understood the appeal of Thousand Island dressing. Besides, isn't it a burger sauce? French and Ranch weren't my faves either, but one day Catalina entered my life and changed everything. It was like French dressing's sassier, spicier cousin—the one with tattoos and an attitude. It was a sweet-and-tangy red elixir that somehow made even the most basic iceberg salad feel more gourmet—at least to me. Suddenly, salads weren't just a mandatory side dish; they were something to look forward to.

Potlucks and family gatherings had their own lineup of salads, with most containing more mayo than vegetables. My mom made all the creamy classics: potato salad (extra dill pickles, of course), coleslaw (with cabbage from our garden) and macaroni salad (with a generous scoop of Miracle Whip and a sprinkle of paprika for that "fancy" touch). These were the salads we gobbled up at every barbecue, every holiday and every family get-together. (Come to think of it, a meal in the '70s wasn't complete unless one dish had mayonnaise binding it together.)

Special occasions meant busting out the four-bean salad or, if you really wanted to impress, you'd serve a molded gelatin "salad" with various canned fruits suspended in its neon wobble. Despite their simplicity—or maybe because of it—those early salads sparked a lifelong love.

Once I got my driver's license in high school, my salad obsession soared to new heights. Borrowing my mom's Ford Granada and with girlfriends Jill, Beth and Stacy in tow, I discovered what felt like the pinnacle of salad innovation at the time: Yup, you guessed it, the Wendy's salad bar. For a mere $3.99, it became our regular lunchtime destination, an all-you-can-eat buffet of chopped romaine, unlimited toppings and oily-but-yummy dressings that we'd pile sky-high on our plates like some type of edible Jenga tower.

I can't say for sure, but I strongly suspect our teenage salad feasts contributed to the eventual shutdown of Wendy's salad bars across the country. You can't turn a profit when teenagers are eating their weight in macaroni, shredded cheddar and ladles of Catalina for under four bucks, can you?

> **The days of boring iceberg with glugs of Catalina are long gone. Welcome to the new era of salads—you're going to love it here.**

Fast forward to today. Salads have seriously leveled up from somewhat forgettable to absolutely fabulous—and I'm here for it! They're no longer *just* side dishes; they're often main events, packed with flavor and full of personality. They're creative, colorful and adventurous, fitting every mood, every craving and every occasion. The days of boring iceberg with glugs of Catalina are long gone (You listening, brother-in-law Gary?). Welcome to the new era of salads—you're going to love it here.

So, what's changed?

Greens got an upgrade: Iceberg has stepped aside for baby arugula, kale, spring mix and every sprout under the sun.

Dressings went DIY: Bottled dressings still exist (and some are really tasty!), but now we whisk up zippy vinaigrettes, "creamy" vegan cashew dressings and bold, herb-infused blends using various wine vinegars and high-quality olive oil instead of plain white vinegar and the suspicious-sounding "salad oil" of the past.

Toppings turned top-notch: Spicy chickpeas, Parmesan shavings, pomegranate seeds, pickled onions, chimichurri—anything goes in today's elevated salad world.

Global flavors took center stage: Salads now feature bold flavors from every corner of the world—Mediterranean, Asian, Middle Eastern, Latin American—you name it.

Grains and proteins joined the party: Quinoa, farro, lentils, grilled steak, shrimp skewers—salads are no longer *just* vegetables.

Oh, and while I'm on the topic of salads having a glow up, have you noticed that kale is currently living its best life? It gets massaged with oil and rubbed with sea salt like it's at a high-end spa, then adorned with the trendiest toppings—roasted edamame, toasted pine nuts and grilled avocado with a lemon-tahini vinaigrette. Kale is basically the Beyoncé of greens with romaine and spinach as the background dancers. There's even a line of merch emblazoned with "Eat More Kale." Spinach could never. (If you're a fan of kale, you're in for a treat with my kale salad recipes. Not keen on kale? You're about to be converted.)

After browsing through the pages of *Every Salad Ever,* some of you will wonder—where's the goat cheese? Well, spoiler alert: It's nowhere. Not in this book, not on my plate, not in my fridge. If you love it, I respect you. But for me? That tangy farmyard-flavored crumble is a firm no, hard pass, immediate eject button. To quote the famous lyrics of Daryl Hall & John Oates, "I can't go for that. No can do." I'd rather lick a goat's face. Tip: I'm guessing that anywhere I use feta, goat cheese would work but, let's be honest, feta *is* the GOAT. (Rant over. Thanks for listening!)

Most of my recipes are fresh, vibrant, healthy and wholesome (look at the photos!), while others are

richer, celebratory and splurge-worthy, since I believe salads can be both whole foods and soul foods. "Whole foods" salads are packed with fresh, nutrient-dense ingredients—leafy greens (not just iceberg!), colorful veggies, hearty grains, fiber-filled beans, nuts or seeds and good fats like those from avocados and olive oil. "Soul foods" salads tend to be creamier, richer, perhaps with cheese or a crumble of crispy bacon, or a pasta-packed potluck pleaser that sparks joy and brings people together. (Speaking of pasta, one night during a bout of insomnia caused by thoughts of this book becoming a complete and utter failure, I took that ridiculous, viral Instagram quiz to determine what pasta shape I am. Fusilli, if you're curious. Thin and twisted. Oh, great.)

Last summer, I finally announced to female friends that I was writing a salad book (I was keeping it a secret), and they all had similar, extremely positive, encouraging reactions: "That's so exciting! I can't wait to get it! I LOVE salads! This is the best news ever!" When I announced to male friends that I was writing a salad book, they'd tilt their heads sideways, pause and reply, "So . . . you mean . . . lettuce-y stuff? Like rabbit food? For losing weight?" LOL. Let me be clear: *Every Salad Ever* is not a diet or weight-loss book. But my recipes can absolutely fit into any healthy-eating plan or weight-loss journey. Consider this book a trusted resource for relatable, reliable, ridiculously tasty recipes for real life. Salad recipes you'll make for potlucks, picnics, dinner parties, backyard BBQs, family celebrations, baby and bridal showers, brunches, weekday lunches, meal-prep Sundays, girls' weekends, beach days, the holidays and random Tuesdays. It's *Every Salad* recipe you'll *Ever* need. Hungry-man salads included.

Whether you're craving a bright, beautiful, fresh summer salad (page 58), a cozy fall creation (page 242) or a showstopping pasta salad that even Joseph Francis Tribbiani Jr. would happily devour (page 116), this jam-packed cookbook (not actually packed with jam) will take your salads to the next level with more than 100 fabulous, flavor-packed recipes for every season and every reason.

Lettuce raise a fork to your new salad obsession!

Greta

Author's Notes

As with all my cookbooks, I've included the nutritional analysis for every salad recipe. But food is more than just calories, fat grams and carb counts—it's comfort, nostalgia, connection, tradition, celebration, a passport to different cultures, a hug in an edible form and a delicious excuse to gather around the table. Please keep in mind that both your body and soul need nourishment!

For those with food allergies, intolerances or special dietary needs, always check the labels of food products that you suspect might not be suitable for you. Products such as vegetable or chicken broth, soy sauce, hoisin sauce, barbecue sauce and taco seasoning (to name a few) may or may not be gluten-free.

Hungry for more?
Introducing SOUND BITES!
Sound Bites are short, snappy audio clips that bring each recipe to life—and you'll find 100 entertaining episodes at everysaladever.com/soundbites. Just click play and I'll be right there with you, dishing out recipe tips, helpful hacks and tasty morsels of culinary "whizdom," served with a side of gourmet giggles. It's like having a cooking buddy in your kitchen, only I won't judge how much feta you're adding.

CHAPTER 1

GRAINY GOODNESS

Hop on the grain train!
Next stop, salad heaven.

THE GRAINS Explained

Brown Rice GF

- Buy quick-cooking (20 minutes) but not instant rice

Jasmine Rice GF

- Fragrant and fluffy
- Softer and a bit stickier than basmati

Wild Rice Blend GF

- Earthy and vibrant
- Usually contains brown, red and black rice

Bulgur Wheat

- Choose coarse (whole-grain) bulgur
- High in fiber
- Similar to brown rice in taste and texture

Pearl Barley

- Slightly chewy, mild flavor
- One of the very first cultivated grains!

Whole Wheat Couscous

- Not actually a grain, but similar usage
- Very easy to cook; basically foolproof

Farro

- Nutty and chewy
- High in fiber
- Look for pearled farro (no need to soak overnight)

Tri-color Quinoa

Quinoa GF

- Technically a seed
- Quick-cooking
- 8 g protein per cup (cooked)

Red Quinoa

White Quinoa

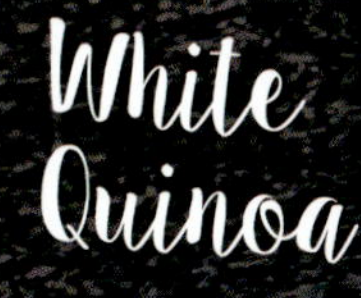

Other salad grains worth exploring: spelt, buckwheat (gluten-free), wheat berries, freekeh.

Grains

Brown Rice Cowboy Caviar Salad

GF DF V

"Cowboy Caviar" is one of the most popular salads for picnics, potlucks, backyard parties and camping trips. I've added brown rice because (1) this ain't my first rodeo and (2) its chewy texture is a perfect complement to the beans, corn and chopped veggies. A hint of spice makes the dressing extra nice!

Salad

3 cups cooked brown rice

1 can (19 oz/540 mL) no-salt-added black beans, drained and rinsed

1 can (19 oz/540 mL) no-salt-added pinto beans, drained and rinsed

1 can (12 oz/340 mL) whole-kernel corn, drained

1 cup diced red bell peppers

1 cup diced green bell peppers

½ cup minced red onions

⅓ cup chopped fresh cilantro (add more if you love it!)

1 jalapeño pepper, seeded and minced

Dressing

⅓ cup olive oil

2 tbsp freshly squeezed lime juice

2 tbsp seasoned rice vinegar

1 tbsp liquid honey (use pure maple syrup for vegan)

1 tsp smoked paprika

1 tsp minced garlic

½ tsp ground cumin

½ tsp sea salt

¼ tsp freshly ground black pepper

Add all salad ingredients to a large bowl and mix well. Set aside.

Whisk together all dressing ingredients in a small bowl or measuring cup (or shake them up in a jar with a lid). Pour dressing over salad and stir until all ingredients are well coated. May be served immediately or stored in the fridge.

If making ahead, add the dressing just before serving. See Kitchen Whizdom for more tips!

Makes about 10 cups salad

Per cup: 146 calories, 7.7 g total fat (1 g saturated fat), 3.8 g protein, 17.1 g carbohydrate (4 g fiber, 3.9 g sugars), 0 mg cholesterol, 126 mg sodium

Some salads taste best at room temperature, and this is one of them. Also, if the salad sits for a day in the fridge, the brown rice will soak up most of the dressing, leaving the salad a bit dry. I'd suggest making one and a half times the dressing recipe and saving some for "refreshing" any leftovers.

SWAP IT

Use farro instead of brown rice. Trade the pinto beans for canned black-eyed peas or lentils.

TOP IT

I love this salad with diced avocados, but don't add them until serving time.

Grains

Mediterranean Farro Salad

with crunchy veggies, chickpeas and feta

Originating in a farro-way place (the Middle East), this chewy, nutty, ancient grain is basically a blank slate for flavor. When paired with Mediterranean salad staples, this plant-based recipe makes a filling, satisfying lunch (use diced avocados instead of feta for vegan). The fresh herbs are essential to this recipe, so please don't leave them out!

Salad

1½ cups uncooked farro (see Kitchen Whizdom)

1 cup quartered grape tomatoes

1 cup peeled, diced English cucumbers

1 cup diced red bell peppers

1 cup canned no-salt-added chickpeas, drained and rinsed

⅓ cup finely diced red onions

⅓ cup toasted pine nuts (optional but recommended)

⅓ cup chopped fresh parsley

2 tbsp minced fresh dill, mint or basil

Dressing

2 tbsp olive oil

2 tbsp freshly squeezed lemon juice

1 tbsp balsamic vinegar

1 tsp liquid honey

½ tsp Dijon mustard

½ tsp dried oregano

½ cup crumbled light or regular feta cheese (2 oz/57 g)

Sea salt and freshly ground black pepper to taste

Place farro in a mesh sieve and rinse well under cold running water. Add rinsed farro to a medium pot with 8 cups salted water. Bring to a boil and cook farro as you would cook pasta, until tender. Farro should still be a bit chewy. Check package for recommended cooking time, anywhere from 10 to 30 minutes, depending on the type of farro you're using. Drain farro and cool completely.

Transfer cooled farro to a large bowl and add tomatoes, cucumbers, bell peppers, chickpeas, onions, pine nuts (if using) and herbs. Set aside.

In a small bowl or measuring cup, whisk together all dressing ingredients until well blended. Pour over salad and mix gently until all ingredients are coated with dressing. Gently stir in feta and season with salt and pepper to taste. May be served immediately or covered and refrigerated before serving. I prefer this salad at room temperature.

Makes about 8 cups salad

Per cup: 206 calories, 5.9 g total fat (1.4 g saturated fat), 8.5 g protein, 32 g carbohydrate (5.7 g fiber, 5.3 g sugars), 3.5 mg cholesterol, 100 mg sodium

Do I really need to rinse farro before cooking? Yes, you do. The grain often has a powdery, dusty coating after harvesting that needs to be removed. A quick rinse in a fine-mesh sieve under cold running water will do the trick.

A timeless
SALAD
using
ANCIENT
GRAINS
SWITCH IT UP
Make this salad gluten-free by using quinoa instead of farro.
JAZZ IT UP
Add ½ cup pitted Kalamata olives. Chopped avocados would also be delicious!

Moroccan Quinoa Salad

with chickpeas, currants and warm spices

GF DF V

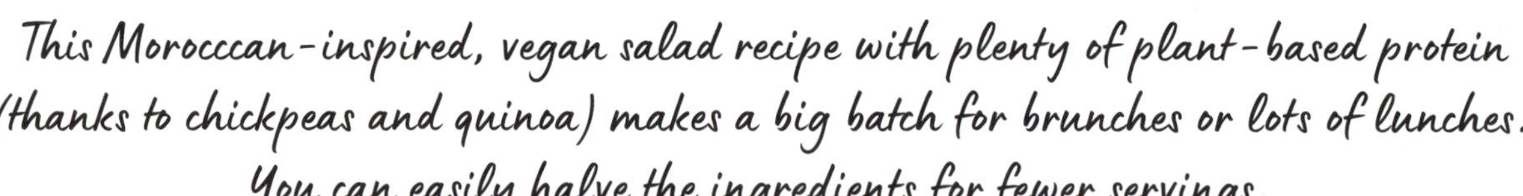

This Morocccan-inspired, vegan salad recipe with plenty of plant-based protein (thanks to chickpeas and quinoa) makes a big batch for brunches or lots of lunches. You can easily halve the ingredients for fewer servings.

2 cups uncooked quinoa, rinsed
3½ cups low-sodium vegetable broth
½ cup dried currants
2 tsp medium curry powder
2 tsp ground cumin
2 tsp liquid honey (or granulated sugar for vegan)
1 tsp ground coriander
½ tsp sea salt
1 can (19 oz/540 mL) no-salt-added chickpeas, drained and rinsed
1 cup each finely chopped red bell peppers, grated carrots and peeled, diced English cucumbers
⅔ cup chopped green onions
¼ cup olive oil
¼ cup freshly squeezed lemon juice
¼ cup minced fresh mint
½ tsp freshly ground black pepper

In a medium pot, combine quinoa, broth, currants, curry powder, cumin, honey, coriander and salt. Bring mixture to a boil. Reduce heat to low, cover and simmer for 12 to 15 minutes, until quinoa is tender and liquid has been absorbed. Remove from heat and let stand, covered, for 10 minutes. Cool completely. (Spread cooked quinoa on a baking sheet to speed up the cooling process.)

Transfer cooled quinoa to a large bowl. Add all remaining ingredients and mix well. Cover and refrigerate for at least 1 or 2 hours before serving. Tastes even better the next day!

Makes about 10 cups salad

Per cup: 267 calories, 8.6 g total fat (1.2 g saturated fat), 8.4 g protein, 41 g carbohydrate (5.9 g fiber, 8.4 g sugars), 0 mg cholesterol, 167 mg sodium

For perfectly cooked quinoa (not mushy, not crunchy), use 1¾ cups liquid (water or broth) per 1 cup quinoa, add a generous pinch of salt, bring to a boil, reduce heat to low (maintain a gentle simmer), then cover and cook until the quinoa has absorbed all the liquid. Cooking time varies depending on quantity, but it'll be anywhere from 12 to 15 minutes. Remove the pot from the heat and let the quinoa sit (covered) for 10 minutes. You're basically moving it from a hot tub to a steam room at this point. All those little curlicues will pop open, resulting in quinoa perfection every time. Fluff the quinoa with a fork and proceed according to the recipe.

SWAP IT
Use tri-color quinoa (red, white, black) instead of regular quinoa.
TOP IT
Sliced, toasted almonds are a tasty, pretty garnish.

Grains

Thai Crunch Quinoa Salad

with the yummiest sesame-peanut dressing

I could eat this salad every day and never get tired of it, since it contains all the elements of a perfect salad: color, crunch, texture, flavor and lip-smacking dressing. I love peanut-flavored ANYTHING. In fact, one time I made just the dressing and ate all of it with a spoon, like soup. Please don't tell anyone. ☺

Salad

1 cup uncooked quinoa, rinsed

1¾ cups low-sodium vegetable broth

1 cup very thinly sliced red cabbage

¾ cup diced red bell peppers

¾ cup grated carrots

¾ cup peeled, diced English cucumbers

¾ cup sugar snap peas, thinly cut on an angle

⅓ cup chopped green onions

¼ to ⅓ cup minced fresh cilantro

Chopped peanuts or cashews for garnish (optional)

Dressing

⅓ cup natural peanut butter

3 tbsp warm water

2 tbsp reduced-sodium soy sauce (use tamari soy sauce for gluten-free)

2 tbsp seasoned rice vinegar

1 tbsp freshly squeezed lime juice

1 tbsp pure maple syrup

2 tsp dark sesame oil

2 tsp grated fresh gingerroot

2 tsp minced garlic

1 tsp Sriracha hot sauce (optional)

Combine quinoa and broth in a medium pot. Bring to a boil over high heat. Reduce heat to low, cover and simmer for 12 to 15 minutes, or until quinoa is tender and liquid has been absorbed. Remove from heat and let stand, covered, for 10 minutes. Cool completely. (Spread cooked quinoa on a baking sheet to speed up the cooling process.)

In a large bowl, stir together cooled quinoa, cabbage, bell peppers, carrots, cucumbers, sugar snap peas, onions and cilantro. Set aside.

In a small bowl, whisk together all dressing ingredients until well blended. (I like to use my small, single-serve blender to make this dressing perfectly smooth.) Pour dressing over salad and mix well. Garnish with chopped nuts and more cilantro, if desired. If making ahead, add the dressing and cilantro just before serving.

Makes about 7 cups salad

Per cup: 208 calories, 8.3 g total fat (1.2 g saturated fat), 7.7 g protein, 26.3 g carbohydrate (3.8 g fiber, 5.9 g sugars), 0 mg cholesterol, 282 mg sodium

TOP IT
Add chopped or sliced cooked chicken breasts for a protein boost.
WARNING: HIGHLY ADDICTIVE
SWAP IT
Replace the sugar snap peas with shelled edamame or green peas.

Barley, Beets & Baby Kale Salad

with creamy maple-balsamic dressing

I would describe this cool-weather side salad as a bit unusual...and that's why I like it! Cook the barley (or just about any grain) in advance to save time. Once the beets are roasted, the salad comes together very quickly. The all-purpose, drool-worthy dressing is worth doubling, so you'll have extra in the fridge to drizzle on salads all week.

Dressing

¼ cup olive oil

3 tbsp balsamic vinegar

2 tbsp mayonnaise

1 to 2 tbsp pure maple syrup

1 tsp minced garlic

1 tsp Dijon mustard

½ tsp sea salt

⅛ tsp freshly ground black pepper

Salad

2 large or 3 medium golden beets (about 1¼ lbs/567 g)

Olive oil

Sea salt and freshly ground black pepper

3 cups cooked pearl barley (see Kitchen Whizdom)

1 big handful baby kale

¾ cup crumbled light or regular feta cheese (3 oz/85 g)

⅓ cup chopped pistachios

Make the dressing: If you have a single-serve blender or mini food processor, now's the time to use it. Whirl all dressing ingredients together until well blended. You can also whisk them together in a small bowl or give them a good shake in a mason jar. Store in the fridge until ready to use.

Preheat oven to 400°F. I prefer peeling golden beets with a vegetable peeler BEFORE roasting. So please do that! Cut the beets in half so they'll roast faster. Place them on a sheet of aluminum foil and drizzle with a bit of olive oil, then sprinkle with salt and pepper. Fold up the foil and wrap beets loosely together, but not touching. Place the beet "packet" on a baking sheet and roast the beets until tender, about 45 minutes, depending on their size. You should be able to pierce through the beets with a fork using light pressure. Remove beets from oven and let cool, then dice them into bite-sized pieces.

Place the cooked barley in a large serving bowl. Add beets, kale, feta, pistachios and half the dressing. Toss using tongs until salad ingredients are well-coated with dressing. Add more dressing until you're happy with how it tastes. Serve immediately, while beets are still warm.

Makes 6 side-dish servings

Per serving: 312 calories, 15.9 g total fat (3.2 g saturated fat), 7.8 g protein, 35.7 g carbohydrate (5.7 g fiber, 10.6 g sugars), 7 mg cholesterol, 517 mg sodium

Though pearl barley isn't a whole grain (it has both the outer husk and bran layer removed), I use it in this recipe because it cooks faster than pot barley and it's readily available at most grocery stores. I refuse to drive all over town looking for ingredients in my old age. (Ha-ha! Okay, I'm not *that* old . . . but my joints ache and I'm in bed by 9 every night. Yes, as a matter of fact, I AM still fun at parties—until precisely 8:45 p.m.) Back to the barley: Since it doesn't have much flavor, I usually cook barley in vegetable or chicken broth. Check the package for exact cooking time and liquid quantity. For some reason, these vary from brand to brand. Let the barley cool to room temperature before mixing it with the other salad ingredients.

SWITCH IT UP

Use quinoa (it's gluten-free!) or farro instead of barley.

JAZZ IT UP

Toss the cooked barley with 2 tbsp minced parsley, dill, basil or cilantro. Use candied pecans instead of pistachios.

Grains

California Quinoa Salad

with mango, coconut and edamame

GF DF V

I love shopping at Whole Foods and I particularly like their California Quinoa Salad, which you'll find on their spectacular salad bar. The flavors, the colors, the crunch! Sadly, the closest Whole Foods is an hour-long drive from my house. Naturally, this meant I had to create my own version of their irresistible salad.

Salad

1 cup uncooked quinoa, rinsed*

1¾ cups low-sodium vegetable broth

1 medium ripe mango, peeled and diced

¾ cup frozen shelled edamame, thawed

¾ cup diced red bell peppers

½ cup sliced almonds

⅓ cup dried currants or chopped raisins

⅓ cup finely minced red onions

⅓ cup unsweetened flaked coconut

3 tbsp minced fresh cilantro

Dressing

2 tbsp olive oil

2 tbsp freshly squeezed lime juice

1 tbsp balsamic vinegar (white or regular)

2 tsp liquid honey (use pure maple syrup for vegan)

Sea salt and freshly ground black pepper to taste

***I use ⅔ cup white quinoa + ⅓ cup red quinoa in this recipe.**

Combine quinoa and broth in a medium pot. Bring to a boil over high heat. Reduce heat to low, cover and simmer for 12 to 15 minutes, or until quinoa is tender and liquid has been absorbed. Remove from heat and let stand, covered, for 10 minutes. Cool completely. (Spread cooked quinoa on a baking sheet to speed up the cooling process.)

In a large bowl, stir together cooled quinoa, mango, edamame, bell peppers, almonds, currants, onions, coconut and cilantro. Set aside.

In a small bowl, whisk together oil, lime juice, vinegar and honey. Pour over salad and mix well. Add salt and pepper to taste and mix again. Chill until cold.

Makes about 6 cups salad

Per cup: 269 calories, 13 g total fat (3 g saturated fat), 7 g protein, 34 g carbohydrate (4.6 g fiber, 13.7 g sugars), 0 mg cholesterol, 101 mg sodium

SWAP IT

Sub green peas for the edamame beans and fresh mint for the cilantro. Not a fan of mango? No problem! Use diced peaches or nectarines.

Perfect for potlucks

TOP IT

Add sliced or diced avocados just before serving.

Whole Wheat Couscous & Cranberry Salad

with almonds, fresh mint and citrus vinaigrette

I'm cuckoo over couscous because it's so simple and quick to cook and it's basically a flavor sponge. This fresh, herby, light-tasting salad reminds me of a pilaf, only better, because it gets drenched with a scrumptious citrus vinaigrette. It's perfect for fall and winter months and would make a tasty addition to any holiday dinner table.

Salad

1½ cups low-sodium vegetable broth

1½ cups uncooked whole wheat couscous

¾ cup peeled, diced English cucumbers

¾ cup diced red bell peppers

½ cup sweetened dried cranberries, chopped

½ cup chopped fresh parsley

⅓ cup minced red onions

⅓ cup sliced almonds, chopped walnuts or chopped pistachios

¼ cup chopped fresh mint

Dressing

⅓ to ½ cup Citrus Vinaigrette (see recipe, page 263)

In a medium pot, bring broth to a boil over high heat. Remove from heat, stir in couscous, cover tightly with a lid and let stand for 5 minutes. Fluff couscous with a fork and let it cool to room temperature. When cool, transfer couscous to a large bowl.

Add cucumbers, bell peppers, cranberries, parsley, onions, almonds and mint to couscous and mix well. Add dressing and mix again. Adjust amount of dressing based on your preference for stronger or milder flavor. May be served immediately at room temperature or covered and stored in the refrigerator to let flavors develop.

Makes about 7 cups salad

Per cup: 237 calories, 7.7 g total fat (0.9 g saturated fat), 5.8 g protein, 36.6 g carbohydrate (3.5 g fiber, 8.7 g sugars), 0 mg cholesterol, 75 mg sodium

Wheat the heck? Did you know couscous is technically not a grain and that it's made from durum wheat ground into flour and mixed with water, just like pasta? It's true! That means you'll never drive by a field of couscous. However, since it's often associated with grains, it's sold in grocery aisles near other grains AND it's made from a grain—it seemed logical to include it here in my Grainy Goodness chapter.

GO cuckoo OVER COUSCOUS

SWITCH IT UP

Bulgur is an excellent substitute for couscous in this recipe.

JAZZ IT UP

For more citrus flavor, add 1 tsp grated orange zest to the salad. Mix well.

1. Rinse.

Take a minute to rinse your grains in a mesh sieve under cold running water to remove any dust, dirt or excess starch.

2. Measure.

Make sure your liquid-to-grain ratio is correct, otherwise you could end up with cooked grains that are crunchy or mushy.

3. Season.

Add salt to your cooking water or, better yet, cook grains in vegetable or chicken broth to amp up their flavor.

4. No peeking, no stirring.

Removing the lid releases steam, disturbing the cooking process, while stirring can activate starches, leaving grains clumpy or sticky. Note: All my pots have glass lids because I absolutely must spy on my food.

Grains of Wisdom:

HOW TO COOK GRAINS LIKE A PRO

Cooked grains can be transformed into an infinite number of delicious salads all year round based on what's in your fridge and what tempts your taste buds. Plus, grain salads are easily packable and portable without getting soggy and wilty, making them perfect for meal prep and desk lunches.

7. Fluff.

Fluff up the grains using a fork to separate them and release excess steam. Now they're ready to eat, unless you've cooked the grains for a salad, in which case . . .

5. Don't overcook.

Grains are done when they're tender but still a bit chewy.

6. Let 'em rest.

Remove the pot from the heat, keep it covered and set a timer for 10 minutes. Go sort socks or scroll Instagram but don't open the lid.

8. Cool.

Spread the hot grains on a parchment-lined baking sheet to speed up the cooling process. Once cool, pick up the parchment and transfer the grains to a mixing bowl. Proceed as directed in the recipe.

The "Rachel Green" Salad

with brown rice, chickpeas and lemony vinaigrette

GF DF V

Grains

*A similar and equally delicious, nutritious, herby grain salad went viral on social media, touted as "The Jennifer Aniston Salad," yet no proof exists that Jen ate it "every day on the set of **Friends**," as the salad's fanatics claimed. I believe it's all fiction, and that's why I'm calling my rendition "The Rachel Green Salad," which seems more appropriate.☺ I've been eating this addictive salad for ages, long before it became an online sensation. Maybe Jen stole my recipe. LOL.*

Dressing

⅓ cup olive oil

3 tbsp freshly squeezed lemon juice

1½ tbsp apple cider vinegar

1 tbsp pure maple syrup or liquid honey

1 tsp grated lemon zest

1 tsp Dijon mustard

½ tsp sea salt

¼ tsp freshly ground black pepper

Salad

2 cups cooked brown rice or quinoa, cooled

1 can (19 oz/540 mL) no-salt-added chickpeas, drained and rinsed

2 cups diced English or mini cucumbers

1 cup crumbled light or regular feta cheese (4 oz/113 g) or 1 medium avocado, diced (for vegan/dairy-free)

½ cup sweetened dried cranberries, chopped

½ cup sliced almonds, toasted

⅓ to ½ cup finely chopped red onions

½ cup chopped fresh flat-leaf parsley

⅓ cup chopped fresh mint

Whisk together all dressing ingredients in a small bowl or measuring cup until well blended. Alternatively, you can shake them up in a mason jar or whirl them in a small blender (I love my portable blender for this purpose). Set aside.

Combine all salad ingredients in a large serving bowl. Add the dressing and mix gently until all ingredients are well coated. Serve immediately or cover and refrigerate until ready to serve. If making ahead, add the parsley and mint just before serving.

Makes about 9 cups salad

Per cup: 268 calories, 13.8 g total fat (2.8 g saturated fat), 8.5 g protein, 29 g carbohydrate (4 g fiber, 6.5 g sugars), 6 mg cholesterol, 299 mg sodium

SWITCH IT UP

Use bulgur wheat or farro instead of brown rice. Try pistachios instead of almonds!

JAZZ IT UP

Want some leafy greens in your Rachel Green salad? Add a small handful of baby arugula.

Holiday Grain Salad

with roasted squash, pomegranate, feta and mint

*

This hearty and healthy recipe isn't just pretty to look at, it's pretty tasty, too! As much as I love and crave salads, sometimes leafy green ones don't cut it in the fall or winter. That's when this colorful salad comes to the rescue. It's an excellent addition to any Thanksgiving or Christmas feast.

Salad

4 cups cubed butternut squash (about ½-inch cubes)

1 tbsp olive oil

4 cups cooked, cooled grains (see Kitchen Whizdom)

1 cup pomegranate seeds

½ cup crumbled light or regular feta cheese (2 oz/57 g)

⅓ cup chopped green onions (with white parts)

⅓ cup chopped fresh parsley

¼ cup chopped fresh mint

Dressing

3 tbsp olive oil

2 tbsp freshly squeezed lemon juice

1 tbsp balsamic vinegar (white or regular)

1 tbsp pure maple syrup

½ tsp Dijon mustard

½ tsp grated orange zest (optional but nice)

Sea salt and freshly ground black pepper

***For gluten-free, grains like quinoa or a combo of brown and wild rice would be perfect.**

Preheat oven to 425°F. In a medium bowl, toss squash cubes with olive oil and a sprinkle of salt and pepper. Spread squash evenly on a small, parchment-lined baking sheet. Roast for 15 to 20 minutes. Give squash a stir halfway through cooking time. Squash should be tender but still have a slight bite. Squishy squash is not good! Remove from oven and let cool.

In a large bowl, combine cooked grains, squash, pomegranate, feta, green onions, parsley and mint. Stir gently to combine. Pretty!

In a small bowl or measuring cup, whisk together all dressing ingredients, except salt and pepper. Pour over salad. Add salt and pepper to taste. A generous grinding of both. Mix well, being careful not to squish the squash. May be served immediately with warm squash or covered and chilled in the refrigerator. I prefer this salad warm or at room temperature.

Makes about 8 cups salad

Per cup: 255 calories, 9.4 g total fat (1.8 g saturated fat), 7.4 g protein, 37 g carbohydrate (5.7 g fiber, 7 g sugars), 3.5 mg cholesterol, 178 mg sodium

You can use just about any grain you prefer in this salad: red and/or white quinoa (technically a seed), wheat berries, farro, bulgur, brown and wild rice combo, mix a bunch together, use couscous . . . whatever! Just make sure you use 4 cups (or so) of COOKED grains and let them cool a bit after cooking. I almost always cook my grains in vegetable broth for a flavor boost. If you look closely at the photo, you'll see I used a combination of farro and quinoa.

TOP IT

Garnish with some roasted, salted pumpkin seeds before serving.

SWAP IT

Can't find pomegranate at the store? Use dried cranberries. Not a fan of squash? Use sweet potatoes.

Copycat Costco Quinoa Salad

with lentils, chopped veggies and lotsa parsley

GF DF V

If you're a Costco member and a salad lover (I am!), then I'm positive their famous quinoa salad has made its way into your cart. I no longer live near Costco, so I created a simplified but equally addictive version of their wildly popular salad. Make it in advance, since it tastes better when the ingredients have time to "marinate" in the fridge. Confession: Sometimes I can't wait and scarf it down immediately.

Salad

1 cup uncooked tri-color quinoa, rinsed

1¾ cups low-sodium vegetable broth

1 cup canned lentils, drained and rinsed

¾ cup peeled, diced English cucumbers (or use those cute little ones!)

¾ cup diced tomatoes (see Kitchen Whizdom)

¾ cup diced red bell peppers

½ cup chopped fresh flat-leaf parsley

¼ cup minced fresh chives

Dressing

¼ cup light-tasting olive oil (see Kitchen Whizdom)

3 tbsp freshly squeezed lemon juice

3 tbsp seasoned rice vinegar

1 tbsp liquid honey (use pure maple syrup for vegan)

1 tsp minced garlic

½ tsp sea salt

⅛ tsp freshly ground black pepper

Combine quinoa and broth in a medium pot. Bring to a boil over high heat. Reduce heat to low, cover and simmer for 12 to 15 minutes, or until quinoa is tender and liquid has been absorbed. Remove from heat and let stand, covered, for 10 minutes. Cool completely. (Spread cooked quinoa on a baking sheet to speed up the cooling process.)

In a large bowl, stir together cooled quinoa, lentils, cucumbers, tomatoes, bell peppers, parsley and chives. Set aside.

In a small bowl or measuring cup, whisk together all dressing ingredients. Pour dressing over salad and stir until all ingredients are well coated. Cover and refrigerate for at least 4 hours before serving (overnight is even better).

Makes about 8 cups salad

Per cup: 167 calories, 6.4 g total fat (0.9 g saturated fat), 5.3 g protein, 22.8 g carbohydrate (3.2 g fiber, 4.3 g sugars), 0 mg cholesterol, 199 mg sodium

Choose Roma (plum) tomatoes or grape tomatoes for this salad and cut them into small pieces. Squeeze out (and discard) the seeds and juice from the plum tomatoes before chopping them up. Cut grape tomatoes into quarters or even smaller pieces. Chop, chop, chop! For the oil, I've subbed light-tasting olive oil for the soybean oil found in the original recipe. If you can't find olive oil labelled "light tasting," use an oil with neutral flavor like organic sunflower or safflower oil.

SWAP IT
Love cilantro? It's perfect in this recipe!
Use 1/3 cup and omit the parsley.
The HERB is superb! Don't leave out the parsley.
TOP IT
Add some crumbled feta
cheese before serving.

Grains

Roasted Sweet Potato Grain Bowls

with tahini-balsamic dressing

GF DF V

What's a grain bowl? It's simply a salad that uses cooked grains as the base instead of traditional salad greens. In this case, I've used a brown-and-wild-rice combo, but quinoa or farro would be great, too. A drizzle of delicious tahini-balsamic dressing will dazzle your taste buds!

Dressing

⅓ cup tahini

3 tbsp white balsamic vinegar

3 tbsp water

1 tbsp freshly squeezed lemon juice

1 tbsp pure maple syrup

1 tsp reduced-sodium soy sauce (use tamari soy sauce for gluten-free)

¼ tsp sea salt

⅛ tsp freshly ground black pepper

Salad

2 cups low-sodium vegetable broth

1 cup uncooked brown-and-wild-rice blend

2 tbsp minced fresh cilantro or parsley

1 large sweet potato (about 1 lb/454 g), peeled and diced

1 medium red onion, cut into 8 wedges

1 tbsp plus 1 tsp olive oil, divided

½ tsp sea salt

¼ tsp freshly ground black pepper

3 large kale leaves, ribs removed, chopped

Whisk together all dressing ingredients in a small bowl or measuring cup until well blended. Thin dressing to desired consistency by adding more water. (I like to use my small, single-serve blender to make this dressing.) Refrigerate until ready to use.

In a medium pot, bring vegetable broth and rice to a boil. Reduce heat to low, cover and simmer until liquid has been absorbed and rice is tender. Check package for suggested cooking time. Remove from heat, stir in cilantro and let rice stand, covered, until ready to use.

Preheat oven to 450°F. Line a medium baking sheet with parchment paper or brush lightly with oil. Set aside.

In a large bowl, toss together sweet potatoes, onion wedges, 1 tbsp olive oil, salt and pepper until vegetables are well coated with seasonings. Spread vegetables in a single layer on prepared baking sheet. Roast for 20 minutes, stirring once halfway through cooking time. Be careful not to burn them.

Meanwhile, massage kale with remaining 1 tsp olive oil and a pinch of salt and pepper until all pieces are softened (use your hands and the bowl from sweet potatoes). Remove baking sheet from oven after 20 minutes, spread kale over sweet potatoes and onions and roast all vegetables for 5 more minutes.

To assemble salad, divide rice mixture among 4 shallow serving bowls. Top with roasted vegetables and drizzle with dressing. Serve immediately.

Makes 4 servings

Per serving: 483 calories, 14.9 g total fat (2.2 g saturated fat), 10.5 g protein, 78 g carbohydrate (8 g fiber, 13 g sugars), 0 mg cholesterol, 643 mg sodium

SWAP IT
Use bulgur, farro or quinoa instead of brown/wild rice.

TOP IT
Sprinkle with feta cheese or diced avocados before serving.

Roasted Veggie Couscous Salad

with feta and fresh herbs

Roast for the most flavor! That's my motto when serving warm vegetables in cooler weather. While the veggies roast, you can prepare the rest of your meal. Or MAKE this a vegetarian meal by adding hearty, healthy chickpeas with their rib-sticking power.

1 large sweet potato (about 1 lb/454 g), peeled and diced

1 large red bell pepper, seeded and chopped

1 large yellow bell pepper, seeded and chopped

1 medium red onion, chopped

1 medium zucchini, chopped

1 large portobello mushroom, chopped

2 tbsp olive oil

1 tbsp balsamic vinegar

1 tbsp minced fresh rosemary or thyme, or a bit of both

2 tsp minced garlic

½ tsp sea salt

¼ tsp freshly ground black pepper

1½ cups low-sodium vegetable broth

1½ cups uncooked whole wheat couscous*

1 tsp grated lemon zest

½ cup crumbled light or regular feta cheese (2 oz/57 g) or ⅓ cup freshly grated Parmesan cheese

¼ cup chopped fresh basil

Olive oil, freshly squeezed lemon juice and freshly ground black pepper to taste

***Make this salad gluten-free by using quinoa instead of couscous. Cook 1 cup quinoa in 1¾ cups vegetable broth.**

Preheat oven to 450°F. Line a very large baking sheet with parchment paper or brush lightly with oil.

In a large bowl, combine sweet potato, red pepper, yellow pepper, onion, zucchini and mushroom. Add olive oil, balsamic vinegar, rosemary, garlic, salt and pepper. Toss or mix well to coat vegetables with seasonings.

Spread vegetable mixture in a single layer on prepared baking sheet. Roast about 25 minutes or until vegetables are tender, stirring once halfway through cooking time.

While vegetables are roasting, make couscous. In a medium pot, bring broth to a boil over high heat. Remove from heat, stir in couscous and lemon zest, cover tightly with lid and let stand for about 10 minutes until ready to use.

In a large serving bowl, combine roasted vegetables with cooked couscous, feta and basil. Add a drizzle of olive oil, a squeeze of lemon juice and a few grinds of black pepper. Serve warm.

Makes about 8 cups salad

Per cup: 237 calories, 5.5 g total fat (1.3 g saturated fat), 7.7 g protein, 38.6 g carbohydrate (4.5 g fiber, 6.4 g sugars), 4 mg cholesterol, 294 mg sodium

ROASTED
VEGETABLES
+
FLUFFY
COUSCOUS
=
happy
belly!

Lemony Quinoa Tabbouleh Salad

with pomegranate, parsley and mint

GF DF 

Traditional Middle Eastern tabbouleh gets a modern upgrade when "superfood" quinoa replaces the usual cracked bulgur wheat. Serve it with grilled kebabs, hummus and pitas, or alone as a salad. Fresh and delish!

Salad

1 cup uncooked quinoa, rinsed (white, red or a combination of both; see Kitchen Whizdom)

1¾ cups low-sodium vegetable broth

½ tsp ground cumin

1 cup peeled, finely diced English cucumbers

1 cup quartered grape tomatoes

½ cup each finely grated carrots and chopped green onions

½ cup pomegranate seeds

½ cup chopped fresh parsley

⅓ cup finely chopped fresh mint

Dressing

2 tbsp olive oil

2 tbsp freshly squeezed lemon juice

1 tsp grated lemon zest

1 tsp minced garlic

1 tsp maple syrup, liquid honey or granulated sugar (optional)

½ tsp sea salt

¼ tsp freshly ground black pepper

In a medium pot, combine quinoa, vegetable broth and cumin. Bring to a boil over high heat. Reduce heat to low, cover and gently simmer for 12 to 15 minutes, until quinoa is tender and liquid has been absorbed. Remove from heat and let stand, covered, for 10 minutes. Cool completely. (Spread cooked quinoa on a baking sheet to speed up the cooling process.)

Transfer cooled quinoa to a mixing bowl. Add cucumbers, tomatoes, carrots, green onions, pomegranate, parsley and mint. Mix well.

In a small bowl, whisk together olive oil, lemon juice, lemon zest, garlic and maple syrup, if using. Pour over salad. Mix well. Add salt and pepper and mix again. Cover and refrigerate for several hours for the best flavor.

Makes about 6 cups salad

Per cup: 147 calories, 6.3 g total fat (0.7 g saturated fat), 4 g protein, 21 g carbohydrate (3 g fiber, 1.3 g sugars), 0 mg cholesterol, 238 mg sodium

If your quinoa isn't the pre-rinsed variety (check the bag or box), then place it in a mesh sieve and rinse it well under cold running water before cooking. I sometimes sub finely diced red bell peppers for the grape tomatoes and the salad tastes just as delicious. (I have a friend who hates raw tomatoes and, despite this nonsensical aversion, I still like her. Jen loves this salad with the bell peppers swap.) Finally, pomegranate can be impossible to find in the middle of summer. Sweetened, dried cranberries are a good replacement—just soak them for 5 minutes in warm water to plump them up before adding.

Pretty with pomegranate

Grains

VIETNAMESE-STYLE

Jasmine Rice Salad

with cucumbers, edamame and cilantro

Inspired by a delicious yet simple lunch I ate in a Vietnamese restaurant, this delicate, pretty salad is one of my personal favorites. I love the scent of jasmine rice cooking because it reminds me of popcorn. Heavenly! Everything in this salad bowl makes me happy: cucumbers and shallots sliced paper-thin, the tangy-sweet dressing, fresh cilantro, honey-roasted peanuts. I mean, come on!

Dressing

3 tbsp freshly squeezed lime juice

2 tbsp neutral-tasting oil (peanut, sunflower or safflower)

2 tbsp seasoned rice vinegar

1 tbsp fish sauce (Thai Kitchen brand is GF)

1 tbsp granulated sugar

1 tsp dark sesame oil

1 tsp grated fresh gingerroot

½ tsp crushed red pepper flakes

Salad

2 cups thinly sliced (paper-thin!) English cucumbers

2 medium shallots, thinly sliced (paper-thin!)

3 cups cooked jasmine rice, cooled

1 cup frozen shelled edamame, thawed

⅓ cup chopped fresh cilantro

⅓ cup chopped honey-roasted peanuts

In a small bowl or measuring cup, whisk together all dressing ingredients until well blended. Set aside.

Are your cucumbers and shallots sliced as thinly as humanly possible? Good. (I wear my reading glasses to get precise slices. LOL.) Place them in a large serving bowl. Pour half the dressing over top, give the cukes and shallots a stir and let them marinate in the dressing for about 15 minutes.

Add all remaining salad ingredients and remaining dressing. Mix well. Garnish with chopped peanuts and serve within an hour. Cover leftovers and store in the fridge. The rice will soak up most of the dressing, but it'll still taste pretty good.

Makes 6 side-dish servings

Per serving: 235 calories, 9.1 g total fat (1 g saturated fat), 6.3 g protein, 32 g carbohydrate (2.1 g fiber, 5.6 g sugars), 0 mg cholesterol, 257 mg sodium

I'm being FINicky here, but please don't omit the fish sauce. Leaving out the fish sauce in a Vietnamese recipe would be like leaving out the feta cheese in a Greek salad. Fish sauce is made from salted anchovies and adds a certain something that can't really be replaced. Public Service Announcement: Do *not* take a whiff of fish sauce once you open the little bottle. You'll find fish sauce near the soy sauce and other Asian goodies like chili paste and red curry paste at the grocery store.

SWAP IT
Use basmati rice instead of jasmine and green peas instead of edamame.
JAZZED-UP JASMINE RICE
TOP IT
This salad tastes SO GOOD with grilled shrimp!

Grains

Tex-Mex Quinoa Salad

with chili-lime dressing

GF DF V

A fiesta of flavors and colors, this healthy, filling quinoa salad is a super side dish for any grilled meats or a satisfying lunch on its own. Leftovers taste even better the next day. Olé!

Salad

1 cup uncooked quinoa, rinsed

1¾ cups low-sodium vegetable broth

1 cup quartered grape tomatoes

1 cup no-salt-added canned black beans, drained and rinsed

1 cup whole-kernel corn (see Kitchen Whizdom)

1 cup diced orange bell peppers

½ cup chopped green onions (with white parts)

1 small jalapeño pepper, seeded and finely minced

3 tbsp minced fresh cilantro

Dressing

3 tbsp freshly squeezed lime juice

2 tbsp olive oil or avocado oil

2 tsp liquid honey (use pure maple syrup for vegan)

½ tsp each ground cumin and chili powder

¼ tsp freshly ground black pepper

1 medium avocado, diced

Combine quinoa and vegetable broth in a medium pot. Bring to a boil over high heat. Reduce heat to low, cover and simmer for 12 to 15 minutes, or until quinoa is tender and liquid has been absorbed. Remove from heat and let stand, covered, for 10 minutes. Cool completely. (Spread cooked quinoa on a baking sheet to speed up the cooling process.)

Transfer cooled quinoa to a large bowl. Add tomatoes, beans, corn, bell peppers, onions, jalapeño and cilantro. Mix well.

Whisk together all dressing ingredients in a small bowl or measuring cup. Pour over salad and mix well. Cover and refrigerate for at least 4 hours. Add diced avocados just before serving.

Makes about 8 cups salad

Per cup: 212 calories, 8.3 g total fat (0.9 g saturated fat), 4.9 g protein, 30 g carbohydrate (6.8 g fiber, 3.9 g sugars), 0 mg cholesterol, 138 mg sodium

You can infuse canned corn with tasty, grilled flavor by charring it in a skillet! Heat 1 tbsp avocado oil or olive oil over medium-high heat and add the drained corn. Stir occasionally until it's lightly toasted. Letting the corn rest without constant stirring will give the kernels time to char on each side.

SWAP IT
Try this recipe with
whole wheat couscous
instead of quinoa.
TOP IT
Tastes great
with grilled shrimp!
GRILLING THE CORN
makes it even tastier

Grains

Greek-Style Bulgur Salad

with fresh herbs and creamy tzatziki

If you're a fan of Middle Eastern tabbouleh salad (see recipe, page 180), then you're already familiar with light and nutty bulgur wheat. In this stunning salad, the plain grain gets a triple-whammy flavor boost with the addition of (1) chopped veggies and fresh herbs, (2) a simple red wine vinaigrette and (3) a bonus dollop of tasty tzatziki sauce. Trifecta perfecta!

Dressing

3 tbsp olive oil

2 tbsp red wine vinegar

1 tbsp freshly squeezed lemon juice

2 tsp liquid honey

1 tsp minced garlic

½ tsp Dijon mustard

½ tsp dried oregano

¼ tsp sea salt

Salad

1 cup uncooked coarse bulgur wheat

1½ cups low-sodium vegetable broth

1½ cups diced English cucumbers

1 cup quartered grape tomatoes

1 cup canned no-salt-added chickpeas, drained and rinsed

½ cup diced red onions

½ cup chopped fresh parsley

3 tbsp minced fresh dill

1 medium avocado, diced (optional)

Tzatziki Sauce (see Kitchen Whizdom for recipe)

Whisk together all dressing ingredients in a small bowl or measuring cup until well blended. Refrigerate until ready to use.

Rinse the bulgur in a mesh sieve under cold running water. Drain well. Bring vegetable broth to a boil in a medium pot. Add bulgur and reduce heat to low. Cover and simmer for about 12 minutes, or until liquid has evaporated and bulgur is tender. Remove from heat, cover and let stand for 10 minutes. Cool completely.

Place cooled bulgur in a large serving bowl. Fluff it up with a fork. Add all remaining salad ingredients except avocado and mix gently. Add the dressing and mix again. At this point, the salad can be stored in the fridge for several hours before serving or served immediately. Add diced avocado, if using, just before serving. Top individual servings with a dollop of tzatziki sauce. Yum!

Makes 8 side-dish servings

Per serving (with 3 tbsp tzatziki): 175 calories, 6 g total fat (0.8 g saturated fat), 7.1 g protein, 24.7 g carbohydrate (4.1 g fiber, 4.9 g sugars), 0.8 mg cholesterol, 263 mg sodium

Make your own tzatziki! Combine the following ingredients in a medium bowl and mix well: 1 cup plain 0% Greek yogurt, ¾ cup unpeeled, grated English cucumbers (pat dry with paper towels), 1 tbsp freshly squeezed lemon juice, 1 tbsp minced fresh dill, 2 tsp liquid honey, 1 tsp minced garlic, ½ tsp sea salt and ¼ tsp freshly ground black pepper. Chill before serving. Delish!

Optional
AVOCADOS
take it
OVER THE TOP!

CHAPTER 2

GREENS GALORE

Fresh and flavorful leafy legends.

Seeing is Beleafing
Feast your eyes on my favorite salad greens!
RADICCHIO
BRUSSELS SPROUTS
BOSTON LETTUCE
BABY KALE
COMMON CURLY KALE
BABY ARUGULA
ROMAINE LETTUCE

SPROUTS
BABY SPINACH
SPRING MIX
WATERCRESS
SAVOY CABBAGE
RED LEAF/GREEN LEAF LETTUCE

Greens

Asian Chopped Chicken Salad

with semi-homemade peanut dressing

Slice and dice your way to an Asian-inspired masterpiece! You'll be rewarded for all your chopping, trust me. This crunchy, colorful, flavor-packed salad is topped with a drool-worthy dressing that'll have you savoring every marvelous morsel and mouthful.

Dressing

⅓ cup light peanut sauce (see Kitchen Whizdom)

¼ cup hoisin sauce

1 tbsp red wine vinegar

1 tbsp dark sesame oil

1 tsp grated fresh gingerroot

Salad

3 cups chopped cooked chicken breast (see Kitchen Whizdom)

2 cups packed chopped Napa cabbage

2 cups packed chopped romaine hearts

1 cup grated carrots

1 cup diced red bell peppers

1 cup coarsely chopped bean sprouts

½ cup chopped green onions

⅓ cup chopped fresh cilantro

⅓ cup chopped peanuts

Whisk together all dressing ingredients in a small bowl or measuring cup. Cover and refrigerate until ready to use.

Toss together all salad ingredients in a large serving bowl. Add half the dressing and toss again. This may be enough dressing for your taste. If not, add more until you're happy with the flavor. Serve immediately.

Makes about 9 cups salad

Per cup: 172 calories, 6.3 g total fat (1.2 g saturated fat), 17.1 g protein, 10.6 g carbohydrate (1.8 g fiber, 7.1 g sugars), 40 mg cholesterol, 306 mg sodium

Look for bottles of peanut sauce where stir-fry sauces are sold at your grocery store. I've tried two different brands, San-J and President's Choice, and my dressing turned out great with both options. To save time, I often pick up a rotisserie chicken and chop up both the light and dark meat for this recipe. Lick-the-plate delicious!

SWAP IT
Prefer to make your own peanut sauce? Try the recipe on page 236.
CHOP 'TIL YOU DROP!
TOP IT
Sprinkle with toasted sesame seeds before serving. Crispy wonton strips would be tasty, too!

Greens

Berry Delicious Summer Salad

with honey-Dijon vinaigrette

Here it is, your new go-to summer salad recipe! Mixed greens with blueberries, strawberries, feta cheese, walnuts and razor-thin red onion slices, topped with a lip-smacking, honey-Dijon dressing. Add some chickpeas or cooked chicken breast for a healthy protein boost.

Salad

1 pkg (5 oz/142 g) mixed greens*

1½ cups sliced fresh strawberries

1 cup fresh blueberries

½ cup walnut pieces

½ cup crumbled light or regular feta cheese (2 oz/57g)

⅓ cup very thinly sliced red onions, soaked **(see Kitchen Whizdom, page 158)**

Dressing

¼ cup olive oil

2 tbsp white balsamic vinegar

2 tbsp freshly squeezed lemon juice

2 tbsp liquid honey

1 tbsp Dijon mustard

⅛ tsp each sea salt and freshly ground black pepper

***This basically amounts to a couple giant handfuls of greens. It's hard to measure greens in cups, so just fill up a really big salad bowl with your favorite leafy greens.**

Place all salad ingredients in a large bowl and set aside.

In a small bowl or measuring cup, whisk together all dressing ingredients until well blended.

Pour dressing over salad, using as much or as little dressing as you like. It's up to you! Toss salad with tongs until all ingredients are well coated with dressing. Serve immediately. (Greens go soggy quickly, so it's best to dress this salad right before serving.)

Makes 6 side-dish servings

Per serving: 165 calories, 11 g total fat (1.5 g saturated fat), 3 g protein, 15 g carbohydrate (2 g fiber, 9.5 g sugars), 0 mg cholesterol, 193 mg sodium

KITCHEN WHIZDOM Your leafy green salads will always be dressed for success if you memorize the simple dressing recipe above. I love it with white balsamic vinegar, but it also tastes great with regular balsamic vinegar, apple cider vinegar, red wine vinegar or white wine vinegar. Adding 1 tsp of finely minced garlic or 1 tbsp of minced shallots gives dressings a tasty kick, and I often use pure maple syrup instead of honey (maple syrup addict here!). Store the dressing in a small jar with a fitted lid, such as a mason jar, so you can easily give it a shake before serving.

SWAP IT

For a vegan salad, replace the feta with diced avocados and the honey with pure maple syrup.

TOP IT

Tastes great with Maple-Roasted Pecans. See recipe, page 76.

Greens

Grilled Romaine Hearts

with creamy lemon-tahini dressing

Don't eye-roll me on this, but grilled romaine is actually delicious. I know, I know, it's just WEIRD to put lettuce on the grill, but hardy romaine hearts can handle the heat! I basically smother my smoky, charred romaine with this divine (oil-free) tahini dressing, then grate some good Parmesan over top. The sautéed, savory chickpeas add plant-based protein and fiber.

Dressing

⅓ cup tahini (see Kitchen Whizdom)

3 tbsp plain 0% Greek yogurt

3 tbsp freshly squeezed lemon juice

1 tbsp pure maple syrup

1 tsp minced garlic

1 tsp Dijon mustard

1 tsp reduced-sodium soy sauce (use tamari soy sauce for gluten-free)

¼ tsp freshly ground black pepper

2 to 4 tbsp water for thinning dressing

3 large romaine hearts, halved lengthwise

1 to 2 tbsp olive oil for brushing romaine or olive oil cooking spray

Sea salt and freshly ground black pepper

⅓ cup freshly grated Parmesan cheese

Savory Chickpeas (optional; see recipe, page 251)

Whisk together all dressing ingredients, except water, in a small bowl until well blended or whirl in a small blender until smooth. Add water, 1 tbsp at a time, and blend again until dressing reaches desired consistency. Set aside.

Preheat grill to medium-high heat. Brush (or spray) cut sides of romaine hearts with oil and season with salt and pepper. Lightly oil grill racks. Grill romaine cut-side down for 1 to 2 minutes, until the lettuce is lightly charred (be careful not to burn it!), then flip over and grill for 1 more minute. Remove the romaine from the grill.

Place grilled romaine on a serving plate and drizzle generously with dressing. Top with Parmesan, freshly ground black pepper and savory chickpeas, if using. Serve immediately.

Note: Dressing will thicken if refrigerated so you'll likely need to thin it a bit with water before serving.

Makes 6 servings

Per serving: 153 calories, 10.2 g total fat (2.1 g saturated fat), 6.6 g protein, 9.2 g carbohydrate (3.3 g fiber, 3.4 g sugars), 4 mg cholesterol, 152 mg sodium

I love the richness, silkiness and creaminess that tahini adds to salad dressings and I find myself using it a lot lately. However, not all tahini is created equal, with brands varying in taste, texture and consistency. Runny (almost pourable) tahini is what you're after, not the thick, pasty stuff. I prefer Soom Foods, Trader Joe's and Tamam brands.

SWAP IT

Not into chickpeas? Make the Panko-Parmesan Crumbs instead (see recipe, page 64).

TOP IT

Leave out the chickpeas and add diced tomatoes plus cooked, chopped bacon. So good!

My Famous Kaleslaw Salad

with apple cider vinaigrette

GF DF V

Why is this recipe famous? Because it's the most popular, most requested, most talked about kale salad recipe ever! Or, at least it seems like it. I can't take it anywhere without someone demanding or begging for the recipe. And the delicious dressing will likely become your go-to vinaigrette for any leafy green salads.

Dressing

⅓ cup olive oil

3 tbsp apple cider vinegar

2 tbsp freshly squeezed lemon juice

2 tbsp Dijon mustard

2 tbsp pure maple syrup

¼ tsp each sea salt and freshly ground black pepper (or to taste)

Salad

4 cups packed chopped kale, ribs removed (see Kitchen Whizdom)

2 cups thinly sliced or grated red cabbage

2 cups grated carrots

1 cup sweetened dried cranberries

¾ cup roasted salted pumpkin seeds

½ cup chopped green onions (with white parts)

⅓ cup chopped fresh parsley

Whisk together all dressing ingredients in a small bowl or measuring cup. Set aside until ready to use.

Place chopped kale in a large bowl. Add 3 tbsp of dressing and massage kale for 2 minutes using your hands. I know this seems weird and cumbersome but just do it, please. ☺ You'll thank me later.

Add all remaining salad ingredients and at least 6 tbsp dressing (or more, if desired; you might not use all of it). Mix well. Cover and refrigerate for at least 1 hour before serving.

Makes about 8 cups salad

Per cup: 229 calories, 12.9 g total fat (2.2 g saturated fat), 5.8 g protein, 27 g carbohydrate (3.8 g fiber, 14.7 g sugars*), 0 mg cholesterol, 154 mg sodium

*Lower the sugar content by using reduced-sugar dried cranberries.

When preparing kale for salads (I use standard curly kale for this recipe), it's important to remove the tough stems and "ribs" down the center of the leaf. Just place a big kale leaf on a cutting board, then fold it in half along the center line (the rib). Use a sharp knife to slice the rib away from the leaf in one fell swoop. Now it's time to chop and massage the kale!

SWAP IT
Try sliced almonds
instead of pumpkin seeds.
TOP IT
Add one large, unpeeled, diced apple. Delicious!
(Delicious as in "yummy." Not as in "Delicious apple."
However, a Delicious apple would be great!)

Bottomless Salad for Olive Us

with splurge-worthy Italian dressing

I was obsessed with Olive Garden's famous bottomless salad when I was in my 20s—and not just because I was broke and it was all-you-can-eat. Remember when they'd freshly grate the Parmesan until you said "When!"? Oh, the simple joys of the '90s! I've made some upgrades in my salad imitation by using toasted panko-Parmesan crumbs instead of chunky croutons, olive oil instead of soybean oil, red wine vinegar instead of plain white and Kalamata olives instead of boring black ones.

Dressing

½ cup light-tasting olive oil

¼ cup red wine vinegar

3 tbsp light mayonnaise

2 tbsp finely grated Parmesan cheese

2 tsp liquid honey or granulated sugar

1 tsp dried Italian seasoning

¼ tsp each onion powder and garlic powder

⅛ tsp freshly ground black pepper

Panko-Parmesan Crumbs

1 tbsp butter

½ cup panko bread crumbs

½ tsp each garlic powder and dried Italian seasoning

⅓ cup freshly grated Parmesan cheese

Salad

8 cups packed chopped romaine hearts

3 Roma (plum) tomatoes, halved lengthwise and chopped

½ cup pitted Kalamata olives

6 pepperoncini peppers, whole or sliced (optional)

½ cup very thinly sliced red onions

Add all dressing ingredients to a small blender or food processor and whirl until smooth and creamy. Refrigerate until ready to use.

To make panko-Parmesan crumbs, melt butter in a small (8-inch) skillet over medium heat. Add the panko crumbs and mix well. Add the garlic powder and Italian seasoning and mix again. Continue to heat the crumb mixture, stirring constantly, until it turns golden brown and toasty. Be careful not to burn it. Transfer the hot crumb mixture to a shallow bowl and stir in the Parmesan. Let crumbs cool while you assemble the salad.

In a large bowl, combine romaine hearts, tomatoes, olives, peppers (if using) and onions. Drizzle half the dressing over the salad and mix well using tongs. Add more dressing, if desired. You might not use all of it. Sprinkle cooled Parmesan crumbs over salad and serve immediately.

Makes 6 side-dish servings

Per serving: 315 calories, 26 g total fat (5.6 g saturated fat), 5.5 g protein, 13 g carbohydrate (3 g fiber, 4.2 g sugars), 11 mg cholesterol, 442 mg sodium

SWAP IT

Use 1 tbsp finely grated onions and 1 tsp minced garlic instead of the powdered versions in the dressing.

TOP IT

Sliced grilled chicken or chopped salami make it a mouthwatering meal.

Greens

BBQ Chopped Chicken Salad

with charred corn and creamy ranch dressing

I would describe this salad as life-changing but, to be honest, no salad is life-changing unless Bradley Cooper is feeding it to me. However, this salad comes close: Grilled chicken, charred sweet corn, black beans, plum tomatoes, fresh cilantro and crisp romaine lettuce, tossed in a homemade creamy ranch dressing and drizzled with sweet-and-smoky barbecue sauce. I'm in love—with Bradley AND this salad!

Dressing

1 cup plain 2% Greek yogurt

½ cup light mayonnaise

¼ cup buttermilk

1 tbsp freshly squeezed lemon juice

1 tbsp dried chives

2 tsp dried dill

2 tsp granulated sugar or liquid honey

1 tsp each dried parsley and garlic powder

½ tsp onion powder

½ tsp each sea salt and freshly ground black pepper

Salad

8 large boneless skinless chicken thighs (2¼ lbs/1 kg)

½ cup your favorite BBQ sauce (+ extra for drizzling)

10 cups chopped romaine lettuce

3 large Roma (plum) tomatoes, chopped

1 can (12 oz/340 mL) whole-kernel corn, drained and charred (see Kitchen Whizdom)

1 cup canned black beans, drained and rinsed

½ cup chopped green onions

⅓ cup chopped fresh cilantro

In a medium bowl, whisk together all dressing ingredients until well blended. Cover and refrigerate for at least 8 hours or overnight for the best flavor.

Preheat grill to medium heat and lightly oil grill racks. Grill chicken thighs for about 6 to 8 minutes per side with lid down. Brush generously with BBQ sauce during last 2 minutes of cooking time. Remove from heat and keep warm.

In a large bowl, combine lettuce, tomatoes, corn, beans and green onions with ½ cup dressing. Mix well using tongs. Add more dressing, if desired. Divide salad among 6 salad bowls. Top with sliced or chopped grilled chicken. Top with a drizzle of BBQ sauce, a sprinkle of cilantro and any of the optional salad toppings (see opposite page).

Makes 6 servings

Per serving: 393 calories, 14 g total fat (3.2 g saturated fat), 37.8 g protein, 29.8 g carbohydrate (5.5 g fiber, 16.3 g sugars), 169 mg cholesterol, 626 mg sodium

Be sure to make the ranch dressing at least 8 hours in advance. It needs some "me time" in the fridge for the flavors to develop. Once refrigerated, it'll be thick like a dip. If you prefer it thinner, whisk in a bit of buttermilk. This recipe makes more dressing than you'll need, but you can keep the leftovers in the fridge for 5 days. For the BBQ sauce, I use Sweet Baby Ray's original recipe. To char the corn, heat some avocado oil or olive oil in a skillet over medium-high heat, add the drained corn and stir occasionally until lightly toasted (it'll make popping sounds!). Letting the corn rest without constant stirring will give the kernels time to char on each side.

Optional Toppings:
Diced avocados
Grated cheddar
Grated Monterey Jack
Tortilla strips
Charred corn tastes
A-maize-ING!

Blueberry, Nectarine & Arugula Salad

with diced avocados and honey-lime dressing

This very pretty, pretty delicious summertime salad combines juicy nectarines and blueberries with peppery arugula, creamy avocados and crunchy "cutecumbers" for a fresh, fruity and fabulous side dish.

Salad

1 pkg (5 oz/142 g) baby arugula

2 cups fresh blueberries

2 cups chopped nectarines (see Kitchen Whizdom)

1½ cups sliced mini cucumbers

½ cup crumbled light or regular feta cheese (2 oz/57 g)

2 tbsp chopped fresh mint or basil

1 large avocado, diced

Dressing

3 tbsp freshly squeezed lime juice

2 tbsp avocado oil

2 tbsp liquid honey (use pure maple syrup for vegan)

1 tbsp white wine vinegar

1 tsp Dijon mustard

¼ tsp sea salt

⅛ tsp freshly ground black pepper

Place all salad ingredients (except avocado) in a large bowl. Set aside.

Whisk together all dressing ingredients in a small bowl or measuring cup until well blended. Taste the dressing and if you prefer it a bit stronger/sharper, add another tablespoon of vinegar. Pour dressing over salad and mix well using tongs. Add diced avocado just before serving.

Makes 6 side-dish servings

Per serving: 196 calories, 11 g total fat (2.2 g saturated fat), 4.4 g protein, 22.3 g carbohydrate (4.4 g fiber, 15 g sugars), 5 mg cholesterol, 243 mg sodium

Nectarines are basically fuzzless peaches and I've always preferred them over their furry cousins because I don't need to peel them. Truth be told, I also have a serious aversion to the fuzz on peaches, which likely stems from my eighth-grade boyfriend thinking he was old enough to grow a beard. Regardless, if you don't have a fuzz phobia like I do, feel free to use peaches in this salad instead of nectarines. Choose stone fruits that are ripe but still firm and not too squishy. If you press your thumb into the skin, it should give a little, the same way you choose an avocado.

SWAP IT
Try baby spinach, baby kale or mixed greens instead of arugula.
TOP IT
Sprinkle with toasted, sliced almonds for a bit of crunch and add sliced, cooked chicken breast for more protein.
Baby "cutecumbers" add crunch

Top 5 Tips for NO-FAIL KALE SALADS

1. Remove the "Ribs."

Those fibrous stems are fine for soups or stir-fries, but in a salad? They're like chewing on a tree branch. Take a minute to strip the leaves from the rib so your salad's tender, not tough.

2. Massage the Kale.

Kale's sturdy leaves benefit from a little TLC. After removing the ribs (and stems), chop the leaves into bite-sized pieces and give them a massage with olive oil or some of the dressing. Rub the leaves between your fingers until they darken and soften. They'll go from tough to tasty in two minutes.

3. Balance the Bitterness.

Kale's earthy flavor shines when paired with sweet or tangy ingredients. Add dried fruits (like cranberries or raisins), chopped pears or apples, plus a drizzle of vinaigrette that's sweetened with maple syrup or honey.

4. Mix and Mingle.

Kale loves company! Mix in ingredients that add crunch: toasted nuts, sunflower or pumpkin seeds, crispy chickpeas, or even crushed croutons. Add robust cheeses like crumbled feta or shaved Parmesan to boost flavor.

5. Let it Sit.

Kale salad tastes better when it's had time to relax after all that massaging and mixing. Wait 20 minutes (or longer) before serving the salad, if possible. Giving the leaves extra time to soak up all that flavor means each bite will be more delicious.

Cannellini, Kale & Avocado Salad

with pumpkin seeds and to-die-for dressing

DF

A few years ago, I tasted a version of this higher-fat-but-healthy-fat salad at Erewhon, Los Angeles' famous upscale food market. I couldn't shovel it into my mouth fast enough! I knew I had to re-create the recipe at home, and I ended up liking my version better than the original. Way to go, Greta! Now, please excuse me while I go bathe in the dressing.

Dressing

⅓ cup olive oil

3 tbsp white balsamic vinegar

2 tbsp freshly squeezed lemon juice

1 tbsp pure maple syrup

2 tsp Dijon mustard

1 tsp minced garlic

¼ tsp each sea salt and freshly ground black pepper

Salad

6 cups packed chopped kale, ribs removed

1 can (19 oz/540 mL) no-salt-added white kidney (cannellini) beans, drained and rinsed

1 large avocado, diced

½ cup roasted salted pumpkin seeds

2 tbsp hemp hearts

Whisk together all dressing ingredients in a small bowl or measuring cup and set aside.

Place chopped kale in a large bowl. Add 3 tbsp dressing and massage kale for 2 minutes using your hands. I know this seems weird and cumbersome but just do it, please. ☺ You'll thank me later.

Add all remaining salad ingredients (except hemp hearts) and remaining dressing. Mix well using tongs. Sprinkle hemp hearts over the salad and serve immediately. This isn't a make-ahead salad—it's best if you combine the dressing and salad ingredients just before serving.

Makes 6 side-dish servings

Per serving: 311 calories, 23 g total fat (3.3 g saturated fat), 10 g protein, 20.5 g carbohydrate (7.6 g fiber, 4.4 g sugars), 0 mg cholesterol, 196 mg sodium

My salad recipes featuring kale use the standard curly kale. It's the easiest to find and often the cheapest. However, if you're a fan of flat-leaf Tuscan kale (sometimes called dinosaur kale) or the reddish Russian kale, go ahead and use them. Baby kale is completely different and, as the name implies, it's simply a younger version of kale with small, tender leaves. Baby kale would be used in leafy green salads the same way you'd use spinach or arugula, but it's not a great choice for this recipe.

SWAP IT
Try sunflower seeds instead
of pumpkin seeds.
PLANT-POWERED
Perfection!
TOP IT
For a non-vegan version,
top with shaved Parmesan or
crumbled feta cheese.

Crunchy Asian Slaw

with sweet-and-savory sesame-ginger dressing

GF DF

V

Lots of texture and beautiful colors make this delicious salad a treat for your eyes AND your taste buds!

Salad

4 cups packed chopped Napa cabbage*
1½ cups grated or finely sliced red cabbage*
1½ cups grated carrots
1 cup finely diced red bell peppers
1 cup julienned sugar snap peas
½ cup chopped green onions
½ cup chopped peanuts
⅓ cup chopped fresh cilantro
2 tbsp toasted sesame seeds (optional)

Dressing

¼ cup hoisin sauce (gluten-free or regular)
2 tbsp sunflower or peanut oil
2 tbsp dark sesame oil
2 tbsp freshly squeezed lime juice
2 tbsp seasoned rice vinegar
1 tbsp grated fresh gingerroot
1 tsp minced garlic
Pinch crushed red pepper flakes (or a few drops hot sauce)

***You can replace the Napa cabbage and red cabbage with bagged coleslaw mix. Look for interesting blends of "slaw mix" in the produce section of your grocery store. I like mixes that include green and red cabbage, carrots, kale and Brussels sprouts.**

In a large bowl, combine all salad ingredients and mix well. Set aside.

Whisk together all dressing ingredients in a small bowl or measuring cup. Pour over salad. Mix well using tongs. Make sure salad is evenly coated with dressing. You can serve it immediately or cover and refrigerate until serving time. (Give the salad a good toss before serving if it's been sitting in the fridge.)

Makes about 8 cups salad

Per cup: 142 calories, 10 g total fat (1.4 g saturated fat), 3 g protein, 11 g carbohydrate (3 g fiber, 6 g sugars), 0 mg cholesterol, 155 mg sodium

SWAP IT
Use chopped almonds or cashews instead of peanuts.
TOP IT
Sliced honey-garlic or teriyaki chicken would take this salad over the top!

Galas, Greens & Gorgonzola

with white balsamic vinaigrette

Thinly sliced Gala apples with mixed greens, shaved Brussels sprouts, maple-roasted pecans and mild blue cheese, topped with a lip-smackin', plate-lickin' white balsamic vinaigrette. Yes, please! Make this impressive salad when company's coming.

Dressing

¼ cup olive oil

2 tbsp white balsamic vinegar

1 tbsp freshly squeezed lemon juice

2 tsp pure maple syrup or liquid honey

½ tsp Dijon mustard

½ tsp minced garlic

¼ tsp each sea salt and freshly ground black pepper

Salad

6 cups packed mixed greens

1½ cups very thinly sliced Brussels sprouts (paper thin)

1 large Gala apple, unpeeled, cored and thinly sliced

½ cup crumbled Gorgonzola cheese (2 oz/57 g)

½ cup Maple-Roasted Pecans (see Kitchen Whizdom)

Whisk together all dressing ingredients in a small bowl or measuring cup. Refrigerate until ready to use. (Whisk again before drizzling on salad.)

Just before serving, place greens, Brussels sprouts, apple slices and cheese in a very large salad bowl. Add dressing and toss or mix well (I use tongs) until all greens are well coated. Top individual servings with roasted pecans. I like to chop or crumble them a bit before sprinkling them on my salad. So tasty!

Makes 6 servings

Per serving: 229 calories, 18 g total fat (3.4 g saturated fat), 4 g protein, 16 g carbohydrate (4.4 g fiber, 8.5 g sugars), 9 mg cholesterol, 300 mg sodium

To make Maple-Roasted Pecans, preheat oven to 325°F and line your smallest baking pan with parchment paper. In a medium bowl, combine 1½ cups pecan halves, 3 tbsp pure maple syrup, 1½ tbsp melted butter or coconut oil, ½ tsp cinnamon and ¼ tsp sea salt. Stir until well blended. Spread coated pecans in a single layer on parchment-lined pan. Bake for 10 minutes, give pecans a quick stir, then bake an additional 7 to 10 minutes MAX. Be VERY careful not to burn them. Let cool completely. Use ½ cup (or more!) roasted pecans in the salad and save the rest for a snack. Or just buy maple-roasted pecans. I'll forgive you!

SWAP IT

Not a fan of blue cheese? Add feta instead.

TOP IT

I put sliced avocados on everything—this salad is no exception!

Greens

Grilled Chicken Souvlaki Salad

with double-duty, doubly delicious marinade

For the men who roll their eyes while declaring "Salad is NOT a meal!"—I present to you this filling, flavorful, fully loaded salad masterpiece for manly appetites. The herby, garlicky souvlaki marinade not only results in the tastiest, juiciest chicken, but also doubles as a delicious dressing to take this meal to the flavor max.

Marinade

½ cup plain 0% Greek yogurt
¼ cup olive oil
3 tbsp freshly squeezed lemon juice
2 tbsp red wine vinegar
1 tbsp liquid honey
1 tbsp minced fresh dill
2 tsp Dijon mustard
2 tsp minced garlic
2 tsp dried oregano
1 tsp dried basil
1 tsp grated lemon zest
½ tsp paprika
½ tsp each sea salt and freshly ground black pepper

4 large boneless skinless chicken breasts (about 2 lbs/907 g)

Salad

2 medium heads romaine lettuce, chopped
2 cups diced English cucumbers
2 cups halved or quartered cherry tomatoes
1 large red onion, thinly sliced
1 cup cubed light or regular feta cheese (4 oz/113 g)
¾ cup pitted Kalamata olives

In a small bowl, whisk together all marinade ingredients until well blended. Cover and refrigerate until ready to use.

Cut chicken into 1½-inch chunks and place in a large, resealable freezer bag. Add half the marinade. Seal bag and turn several times to coat chicken with marinade. Refrigerate for at least 8 hours or overnight for the best flavor. Refrigerate remaining marinade to use as the salad dressing.

Preheat grill to medium-high heat. Prep all salad ingredients and place them in a large serving bowl so they're ready to go. Thread chicken onto skewers (discard the used marinade). Gah! I hate this part. Kinda messy.

Lightly oil grill racks. Place skewers onto racks and grill for 10 to 12 minutes, turning occasionally to ensure even cooking. Remove from grill, slide cooked chicken off skewers and add them to the salad. Pour reserved dressing over salad and mix well using tongs. Serve immediately.

Makes 6 servings

Per serving: 391 calories, 19 g total fat (4.8 g saturated fat), 42.4 g protein, 12.8 g carbohydrate (3.4 g fiber, 7.6 g sugars), 129 mg cholesterol, 817 mg sodium

SWITCH IT UP
Trade the romaine lettuce
for any type of salad
greens you love.
JAZZ IT UP
Thickly slice the
red onion and grill the
rings with the chicken
skewers. Delish!

Greens

Kale & Quinoa Power Salad

with broccoli, pears and Parmesan

What makes this a power salad? Well, it's so tasty and addictive, you'll need incredible willpower to resist scarfing back the entire bowlful! I love this type of salad—the kind that's loaded with interesting textures, colors and flavors—with ingredients chopped super small, then dressed with a simple (but so tasty!) white balsamic vinaigrette that hides in all the nooks and crannies.

Dressing

⅓ cup olive oil

¼ cup white balsamic vinegar

1 tbsp freshly squeezed lemon juice

1 tbsp pure maple syrup

1 tsp Dijon mustard

¼ tsp each sea salt and freshly ground black pepper (or to taste)

Salad

6 cups packed chopped kale, ribs removed

2 cups cooked quinoa, cooled

2 cups chopped broccoli florets and stems

2 ripe medium Bartlett pears, diced

1 cup diced red bell peppers

½ cup minced red onions

⅓ cup roasted salted sunflower seeds

⅓ cup freshly grated Parmesan cheese

Whisk together all dressing ingredients in a small bowl or measuring cup and set aside.

Place chopped kale in a large bowl. Add 3 tbsp dressing and massage kale for 2 minutes using your hands. I know this seems weird and cumbersome but just do it, please. ☺ You'll thank me later.

Add all remaining salad ingredients and remaining dressing. Mix well. Cover and refrigerate for at least 1 hour before serving.

Makes about 12 cups salad

Per cup: 168 calories, 9.6 g total fat (1.6 g saturated fat), 4.4 g protein, 16.9 g carbohydrate (2.9 g fiber, 6.6 g sugars), 2 mg cholesterol, 110 mg sodium

SWAP IT

Try pumpkin seeds or chopped pistachios instead of sunflower seeds.

TOP IT

Sprinkle with pomegranate seeds to add some dazzle for a special occasion.

Chicken, Strawberry & Avocado Salad

with baby spinach and citrus vinaigrette

I often blend spinach, strawberries and avocados in my healthy morning smoothies, and that inspired me to create this beautiful, simple, early summer salad (when strawberries are tastiest!). I never get tired of eating it. So delicious and so gorgeous!

Dressing

¼ cup light-tasting olive oil

¼ cup freshly squeezed orange juice

2 tbsp freshly squeezed lemon juice

2 tbsp Dijon mustard

1 tbsp apple cider vinegar

1 tbsp liquid honey

1 tsp grated orange zest

1 tsp grated fresh gingerroot (do not use dried)

¼ tsp each sea salt and freshly ground black pepper

2 tsp poppy seeds

Salad

1 pkg (5 oz/142 g) fresh baby spinach

2 cups sliced fresh strawberries (the fresher, the better!)

2 cups chopped cooked chicken breast

1 cup peeled, diced English cucumbers

1 large avocado, diced

⅓ cup sliced almonds, lightly toasted

⅓ cup very thinly sliced red onions

½ cup crumbled light or regular feta cheese (2 oz/ 57g; optional—use vegan feta for dairy-free)

Add all dressing ingredients except poppy seeds to a blender and whirl until emulsified. A small Magic Bullet, Ninja or BlendJet blender works great for this purpose. Stir in poppy seeds and refrigerate until serving time. Give the dressing a good stir, shake or whisk before using.

Place all salad ingredients in a large bowl. Add half the dressing and mix gently using tongs, being careful not to squish the avocado. Add more dressing to your liking and top with feta, if using. Serve immediately. Or, in my case, grab a fork and eat the whole bowlful!

Makes 6 servings

Per serving: 275 calories, 18.7 g total fat (2.9 g saturated fat), 15.4 g protein, 15 g carbohydrate (4 g fiber, 8 g sugars), 32 mg cholesterol, 238 mg sodium

SWITCH IT UP
Use baby kale or mixed greens instead of baby spinach.
Big BOWL-O-YUM!
JAZZ IT UP
Add 2 tbsp mayonnaise or plain Greek yogurt to the dressing for a creamy variation.

Greens

Chicken & Mango Salad

with sesame-ginger dressing

GF DF

My love of mangoes was solidified when, while vacationing in Costa Rica, a ripe mango fell from a tree and hit me square on the head. It was the tastiest, sweetest, most perfect mango I'd ever eaten. In Isaac Newton-like fashion, this fruitful event sparked a "Eureka!" recipe moment that led to the creation of this mango-licious chicken salad.

Dressing

¼ cup neutral-tasting oil, such as sunflower or safflower oil (I use organic)

3 tbsp seasoned rice vinegar

2 tbsp dark sesame oil

1 tbsp liquid honey

1 tbsp reduced-sodium soy sauce (use tamari soy sauce for gluten-free)

2 tsp grated fresh gingerroot

1 tsp minced garlic

¼ tsp sea salt

⅛ tsp crushed red pepper flakes (optional)

Salad

1 large ripe mango, peeled and thinly sliced

1 large red bell pepper, thinly sliced

1 cup packed grated carrots

½ cup very thinly sliced red onions

⅓ cup coarsely chopped fresh cilantro

6 cups packed mixed greens

3 medium chicken breasts, cooked and thinly sliced or chopped

Chopped cashews, peanuts or toasted sesame seeds for garnish (optional)

Whisk together all dressing ingredients in a small bowl or measuring cup. Refrigerate until ready to use. For a "creamier," smoother dressing, whirl all dressing ingredients in a small blender for about 10 seconds.

In a large bowl, combine mangoes, bell pepper, carrots, onions and cilantro. Mix well. Add 3 tbsp dressing and mix again (using tongs works well).

Arrange greens over bottom of 6 serving plates or bowls. Mound mango mixture on greens. Top with sliced chicken. Drizzle more dressing over the chicken. You might not use all of it. Garnish with chopped cashews, if using, and serve immediately. (Alternatively, you can toss everything together in a large bowl: the mango mixture, greens, chicken, dressing and nuts.)

Makes 6 servings

Per serving: 282 calories, 16 g total fat (1.9 g saturated fat), 17 g protein, 21 g carbohydrate (3.6 g fiber, 15 g sugars), 40 mg cholesterol, 243 mg sodium

SWITCH IT UP
For a vegan option, replace the chicken with sliced avocados and the honey with pure maple syrup.
Try this dressing as a MARINADE FOR SALMON!
JAZZ IT UP
For a slightly thicker, richer dressing, add 2 tbsp peanut butter.

Greens

Kale, Brussels Sprouts & Broccoli Slaw

with creamy orange-poppy seed dressing

Meet your new salad bestie! This popular, chopped green salad with a deliciously creamy, slightly sweet poppy seed dressing is loved by everyone and suits any occasion. If you can, make the dressing a day in advance, since it tastes better when chilled.

Dressing

¾ cup light mayonnaise

2 tbsp freshly squeezed orange juice*

1½ tbsp apple cider vinegar

1 tbsp granulated sugar, liquid honey or pure maple syrup

½ tsp grated orange zest

¼ tsp sea salt

⅛ tsp freshly ground black pepper

1 to 2 tsp poppy seeds

Salad

1 bag (12 oz/340 g) broccoli slaw mix

2 cups packed finely chopped kale, ribs removed

2 cups very thinly sliced Brussels sprouts (paper thin)

1 cup sweetened dried cranberries

¾ cup roasted salted pumpkin seeds

***Buy a small navel orange to get the juice and zest you need for this recipe.**

Make the dressing: Whisk together all dressing ingredients in a small bowl or measuring cup until well blended. I like to use my single-serve blender for this dressing, stirring in the poppy seeds after blending. Cover and refrigerate until ready to use.

Combine all salad ingredients in a large bowl. It's a pretty big salad! Add the dressing and mix well using tongs, until all ingredients are well coated with dressing. Cover and refrigerate at least 1 hour before serving so the kale has time to soften and the veggies get a chance to mingle with the dressing.

Makes about 9 cups salad

Per cup: 172 calories, 10.6 g total fat (1.2 g saturated fat), 4.2 g protein, 18 g carbohydrate (2.9 g fiber, 10 g sugars), 0 mg cholesterol, 270 mg sodium

Why bother with the ubiquitous, food-factory, bagged version of this salad when it's so easy to make fresh at home? Choose readily available curly kale for this salad and don't forget to slice away the tough "ribs" from the leaves before chopping. Broccoli slaw mix has grated carrots and red cabbage added, which make the salad colorful. Look for broccoli slaw mix where you find bags of traditional coleslaw and grab 8 to 10 medium Brussels sprouts while you're at it. That should be plenty. I thinly slice my Brussels sprouts by hand, meticulously, wearing my reading glasses—but I'm kinda weird. You can use a food processor or mandoline slicer if you prefer.

SWAP IT

Sliced almonds or sunflower seeds are good subs for the pumpkin seeds.

TOP IT

Save some cranberries and pumpkin seeds to sprinkle on the salad before serving. Pretty!

Salmon, Avocado & Orange Salad

with ridiculously tasty sesame-ginger dressing

This is definitely not a boring, lettuce-cucumber-tomato-bottled-dressing sad salad situation! Bursting with flavor and loaded with color, texture and healthy fats, this gorgeous meal is sure to impress in any season.

Dressing

¼ cup hoisin sauce*

2 tbsp sunflower or peanut oil

2 tbsp dark sesame oil

2 tbsp freshly squeezed lime juice

2 tbsp seasoned rice vinegar

1 tbsp grated fresh gingerroot

1 tsp minced garlic

1 tsp grated orange zest

Pinch crushed red pepper flakes (or a few drops hot sauce)

Salad

4 boneless skinless salmon fillets, about 6 oz (170 g) each

Sea salt and freshly ground black pepper

1 tbsp olive oil

8 cups packed mixed greens (I use spring mix + sprouts)

2 medium navel oranges, peeled and sliced

1½ cups thinly sliced English cucumbers

1 medium avocado, sliced or diced

1 small red onion, thinly sliced

Toasted sesame seeds and chopped green onions for garnish (optional)

***If gluten-free is important to you, look for gluten-free hoisin sauce. The popular Lee Kum Kee brand makes a GF version, plus there are several brands available online.**

Whisk together all dressing ingredients in a small bowl or measuring cup. Cover and refrigerate until ready to use.

Season salmon fillets with salt and a few grinds of black pepper. Heat olive oil in a 12-inch nonstick skillet over medium-high heat. Add salmon and cook for 3 to 4 minutes, until pieces are lightly browned and crispy. Don't fuss with the salmon. Leaving the pieces untouched in hot oil ensures a beautiful, golden crust.

Carefully turn fillets, reduce heat to medium and continue to cook for 4 to 5 minutes, or until desired doneness. Remove salmon from heat.

While salmon is cooking, arrange greens, oranges, cucumbers, avocado and onion in 4 shallow salad (or pasta) bowls. Put your multitasking skills to use and keep a close eye on the salmon while you arrange those pretty salads!

Top individual salads with cooked salmon and drizzle generously with dressing. Top with sesame seeds and green onions, if using. Serve immediately.

Makes 4 servings

Per serving: 620 calories, 39 g total fat (6.4 g saturated fat), 37.3 g protein, 28.8 g carbohydrate (5.7 g fiber, 18 g sugars), 75 mg cholesterol, 674 mg sodium

SWAP IT
Try sliced, grilled steak or crispy tofu instead of seared salmon.

TOP IT
Sliced or slivered almonds would add some crunch!

Greens

Shaved Brussels Sprouts Salad

with blueberries, avocados and almonds

Let's hear it for Brussels sprouts! Raw, raw, raw! Not gonna lie, I used to hate Brussels sprouts. Now I can't get enough of them, especially thinly shaved in salads. And when blueberries are at their best, this salad beats the rest! It's simple, pretty and full of flavor, thanks to a perfect mix of texture, crunch and sweetness—all dressed up in a light, bright, white balsamic dressing.

Dressing

⅓ cup olive oil

3 tbsp white balsamic vinegar

2 tbsp freshly squeezed lemon juice

1 tbsp pure maple syrup

2 tsp Dijon mustard

1 tsp minced garlic

¼ tsp each sea salt and freshly ground black pepper

Salad

1½ lbs (680 g) Brussels sprouts, thinly shaved

2 cups fresh blueberries

1 cup sliced almonds, lightly toasted

1 large avocado, diced

⅓ cup crumbled light or regular feta cheese (1.5 oz/42 g)

Make the dressing: Whisk together all dressing ingredients in a small bowl or measuring cup until well blended. (Alternatively, you can shake them up in a mason jar or whirl them in a small blender.) Set aside.

Combine all salad ingredients in a large bowl and mix gently to avoid squishing the avocado. Add the dressing and mix again, until all ingredients are well coated. Serve immediately or, to make ahead, leave out the avocado, then dice it up and add just before serving. Brussels sprouts don't get soggy quickly like regular salad greens and taste even better when they've had some time to drink up the dressing.

Makes about 12 cups salad

Per cup: 165 calories, 11.5 g total fat (1.7 g saturated fat), 4.8 g protein, 13.2 g carbohydrate (4.1 g fiber, 5.9 g sugars), 2 mg cholesterol, 128 mg sodium

SWAP IT

For a fall/winter variation, use diced apples instead of blueberries and chopped, toasted (or candied) walnuts or pecans instead of almonds.

TOP IT

Omit the feta and top individual servings with shaved Parmesan.

CHAPTER 3

PASTA PALOOZA

Oodles of noodle salads.

The Pastabilities are Endless!

Whole Wheat Penne

Ditali

GLUTEN-FREE PENNE

Lentil Pasta (various shapes)

Farfalle (Bow Ties)

Tri-Color Rotini
Chickpea Rotini
High-Fiber Rotini
Orzo
Quinoa or Brown Rice Spaghetti
Buckwheat Spaghetti
Whole-Grain Spaghetti
MEDIUM SHELLS

Pasta

Greek Penne Pasta Salad

with feta, olives and fresh oregano

*

If you find yourself saying, "It's all Greek to me," then you must be talking about this incredible-tasting pasta and vegetable medley! Fresh and filling, it's the perfect addition to your backyard BBQ party.

Salad

1 pkg (13 oz/375 g) whole wheat penne*

1½ cups halved cherry or grape tomatoes

1½ cups diced cucumbers (I like mini cucumbers here)

1 cup crumbled light or regular feta cheese (4 oz/113 g)

½ cup thinly sliced red onions

½ cup whole or sliced Kalamata olives

⅓ cup chopped green onions

2 tbsp minced fresh oregano

Dressing

¼ cup olive oil

¼ cup red wine vinegar

1 tbsp freshly squeezed lemon juice

1 tbsp liquid honey

1 tsp Dijon mustard

1 tsp minced garlic

½ tsp dried basil

¼ tsp freshly ground black pepper

***For a gluten-free option, use GF penne or rotini.**

Cook penne according to package directions. Drain, rinse with cold water (to stop the cooking action) and drain again. Transfer pasta to a very large bowl.

Add tomatoes, cucumbers, feta, red onions, olives, green onions and oregano. Mix well.

Make the dressing: Whisk together all dressing ingredients in small bowl or measuring cup. Alternatively, whirl dressing ingredients in a small blender or shake them up in a jar. Pour over salad and mix until penne and vegetables are well coated.

Cover and refrigerate for at least 1 hour before serving. Tastes great the next day, too!

Makes about 16 cups salad

Per cup: 158 calories, 6.2 g total fat (1.5 g saturated fat), 5 g protein, 20 g carbohydrate (2.4 g fiber, 2.3 g sugars), 4 mg cholesterol, 184 mg sodium

When making pasta salad, I often multiply the dressing ingredients by 1.5 so I'll have extra dressing stored in the fridge. Small jars with lids are great for this purpose. I use a splash of extra dressing to freshen up leftover pasta salad that's become a bit dry. This way, I can enjoy my delicious salad before it's *pasta* point of no return!

SWAP IT

Don't have fresh oregano? Add 1 tsp dried oregano to the dressing.

TOP IT

Garnish with some extra crumbled feta and a few grinds of black pepper.

Pasta

Asian Beef Noodle Salad

with grilled steak and whole-grain spaghetti

GF * DF

Oodles of beef and noodles are paired with colorful veggies and a lip-smacking, Asian dressing. My test-kitchen dummies (also known as my neighbors!) rated this salad a 10/10.

Dressing

⅓ cup hoisin sauce

2 tbsp sunflower or peanut oil

2 tbsp dark sesame oil

2 tbsp freshly squeezed lime juice

2 tbsp seasoned rice vinegar

1 tbsp grated fresh gingerroot

1 tsp minced garlic

1 tsp grated orange zest

Pinch crushed red pepper flakes (or a few drops hot sauce)

Salad

10 oz (285 g) uncooked whole-grain spaghetti*

1¼ lbs (567 g) sirloin or striploin steak, grilled and thinly sliced

2 cups small broccoli florets

1 cup peeled, diced English cucumbers

1 cup thinly sliced red bell peppers

1 cup frozen green peas, thawed

½ cup chopped green onions

⅓ cup chopped fresh cilantro or basil (or a bit of both)

Toasted sesame seeds for garnish (optional)

***If gluten-free is important to you, try quinoa spaghetti or other gluten-free noodles and buy gluten-free hoisin sauce. The popular Lee Kum Kee brand makes a GF version.**

Whisk together all dressing ingredients in a small bowl or measuring cup. Cover and refrigerate until ready to use.

Cook spaghetti according to package directions. Drain, rinse with cold water (to stop the cooking action) and drain again. Transfer spaghetti to a large bowl.

Add remaining salad ingredients to cooked spaghetti and mix well using tongs. Add the dressing and mix again, until all ingredients are well coated. Serve immediately or cover and refrigerate until ready to serve. Sprinkle with sesame seeds just before serving, if using.

Makes 4 to 6 servings

Per serving (based on 6 servings): 495 calories, 17.3 g total fat (4 g saturated fat), 31 g protein, 55 g carbohydrate (3.6 g fiber, 12 g sugars), 66 mg cholesterol, 555 mg sodium

SWAP IT
Try shelled edamame instead of green peas.
TOP IT
Dress up the salad with some chopped peanuts or cashews.

Chicken Caprese Pasta Salad

with plump rotini, juicy tomatoes and fresh basil

GF

Inspired by one of my favorite Italian classics, the Caprese salad (see recipe, page 172), this recipe is simple, satisfying and seriously scrumptious. I've written it as a cold salad but, after heating up the leftovers, I discovered it tastes great served warm, too, with the fresh mozzarella a little soft and melty.

Salad

1 pkg (13 oz/375 g) uncooked rotini (gluten-free, regular or whole wheat)

3 cups chopped cooked chicken breast (see Kitchen Whizdom for cooking tips)

2 cups halved cherry tomatoes

1 tub (7 oz/200 g) mini bocconcini (fresh mozzarella), drained

½ cup chopped fresh basil

Dressing

3 tbsp olive oil

3 tbsp balsamic vinegar

2 tbsp plain 0% Greek yogurt or mayonnaise

1 tbsp freshly squeezed lemon juice

1 tbsp pure maple syrup

1 tsp Dijon mustard

1 tsp minced garlic

½ tsp each dried oregano and dried basil

¼ tsp sea salt

⅛ tsp freshly ground black pepper

Cook rotini according to package directions. Drain, rinse with cold water (to stop the cooking action) and drain again. Transfer rotini to a very large bowl.

Add chicken, tomatoes, bocconcini and basil. Mix well.

Whisk together all dressing ingredients in a small bowl or measuring cup. Pour over salad and mix until all ingredients are well coated. Serve immediately or refrigerate for a few hours before serving.

Note: If you're making this ahead, I'd suggest chopping and adding the fresh basil right before serving to avoid a wilty-herb situation. Also, save a bit of the dressing and stir it in at the last minute so the noodles won't be dry.

Makes about 12 cups salad

Per cup: 258 calories, 8.5 g total fat (2.9 g saturated fat), 18.3 g protein, 25.6 g carbohydrate (2.6 g fiber, 2.8 g sugars) 41 mg cholesterol, 188 mg sodium

My go-to, no-hassle cooked chicken choice is a rotisserie chicken from my grocery store. I chop up all the breast meat and use it in this recipe and others that call for precooked chicken. Choose any type of cooked chicken breast you prefer, whether poached, grilled or baked. Want more ideas? Check out my five favorite, flavor-packed chicken marinades on pages 264–265.

SWAP IT

Cutting back on carbs? Replace half the pasta with leafy greens.

TOP IT

Avocado lover? Dice up a medium avocado and add it just before serving.

Karmic Kale Pasta Salad

with tahini-balsamic dressing

DF 

It's food for the soul in a big-batch bowl! With comforting, nourishing ingredients like earthy kale, creamy avocado, hearty chickpeas and a dreamy tahini-balsamic dressing, this feel-good salad was destined for deliciousness.

Salad

4 cups packed chopped kale, ribs removed

1 tbsp olive oil

8 oz (227 g) uncooked gemelli or fusilli

1 can (19 oz/540 mL) no-salt-added chickpeas, drained and rinsed

1½ cups halved or quartered cherry tomatoes

½ cup very thinly sliced red onions*

1 large avocado, diced

½ cup freshly grated or shaved Parmesan cheese (use vegan Parmesan for vegan/dairy-free)

Dressing

⅓ cup olive oil

3 tbsp balsamic vinegar

2 tbsp freshly squeezed lemon juice

2 tbsp tahini

1 to 2 tsp pure maple syrup

1 tsp minced garlic

½ tsp dried basil

½ tsp sea salt

¼ tsp freshly ground black pepper

***Soaking sliced onions in ice water for 20 minutes helps mellow their sharp flavor.**

Add kale to a large bowl and drizzle with olive oil. Using your hands, massage kale for 2 minutes to soften it. This step is important, so don't skip it. Set aside.

Cook gemelli according to package directions. Drain, rinse with cold water (to stop the cooking action) and drain again. Transfer cooked pasta to the bowl with kale. Add chickpeas, tomatoes and onions. Set aside.

Whisk together all dressing ingredients in a small bowl or measuring cup until well blended or, for the best result, whirl ingredients in a mini blender until smooth and creamy. Pour over pasta salad and mix using tongs until all ingredients are well coated. Add avocado and Parmesan and mix again. Top with several grinds of black pepper and serve immediately or refrigerate until serving time. If making ahead, add the avocado and Parmesan right before serving.

Makes about 9 cups salad

Per cup: 315 calories, 15.4 g total fat (2.9 g saturated fat), 9.2 g protein, 33.2 g carbohydrate (6.2 g fiber, 2.8 g sugars), 3 mg cholesterol, 193 mg sodium

SWAP IT

Use light mayonnaise instead of tahini in the dressing (non-vegan).

TOP IT

Sprinkle with 1/4 cup crushed garlicky croutons before serving.

Pasta

Chicken, Mandarin & Avocado Pasta Salad

with toasted almonds and light, creamy dressing

Chopped chicken breasts, oranges and avocados might seem like an unusual pasta salad trio, but they're a match made in flavor heaven. I love the uniqueness (and prettiness) of this salad. It's best eaten immediately after adding the dressing to prevent the salad from drying out.

Dressing

¾ cup plain 0% Greek yogurt

¼ cup mayonnaise (light or regular)

1½ tbsp apple cider vinegar

1 tbsp liquid honey

1 tsp poppy seeds

1 tsp grated orange zest

¼ tsp sea salt

⅛ tsp freshly ground black pepper

Salad

8 oz (227 g) uncooked rotini*

2 cups chopped cooked chicken breasts

1½ cups seedless mandarin orange segments (see Kitchen Whizdom)

1 cup diced celery

1 medium avocado, sliced or diced

½ cup sliced almonds, lightly toasted

¼ cup chopped fresh parsley

***Try high-fiber or whole-grain rotini.**

Whisk together all dressing ingredients in a small bowl. Cover and refrigerate until ready to use.

Cook rotini according to package directions. Drain, rinse with cold water (to stop the cooking action) and drain again. Transfer rotini to a large bowl.

Add remaining salad ingredients to cooked rotini and mix well. Add the dressing and mix again, until all ingredients are well coated. Add some freshly ground black pepper, if desired, and serve immediately.

Note: If making in advance, keep the dressing separate and add it just before serving, otherwise the salad may dry out.

Makes about 10 cups salad

Per cup: 221 calories, 6.9 g total fat (0.9 g saturated fat), 15 g protein, 25.5 g carbohydrate (4.3 g fiber, 5.9 g sugars), 24 mg cholesterol, 107 mg sodium

Though fresh is best, feel free to use canned mandarin orange segments for this salad. They're a little soft and a bit wimpy, but they still work! When shopping for fresh, look for the smallest mandarins (or clementines) and make SURE they're seedless. After peeling, I just patiently pick off any white pith (there really isn't much) before adding the segments to the salad, but I don't obsess about it. It's not like I'm serving the Princess of Wales.

Pasta

Crunchy Peanutty Noodle Salad

with brown rice spaghetti

I could eat peanut sauce every day and never get tired of it! Tossing skinny noodles with healthy, crunchy veggies, piles of cilantro (sorry, cilantro haters!) and decadent, delicious peanut sauce makes for a feel-good, satisfying meal. Want more protein? Add cooked, shredded chicken, shrimp or crispy tofu.

Dressing

⅓ cup natural peanut butter

3 tbsp warm water

2 tbsp reduced-sodium soy sauce (use tamari soy sauce for gluten-free)

2 tbsp seasoned rice vinegar

2 tbsp freshly squeezed lime juice

2 tbsp pure maple syrup

1 tbsp dark sesame oil

2 tsp grated fresh gingerroot

2 tsp minced garlic

¼ tsp crushed red pepper flakes

Salad

8 oz (227 g) uncooked brown rice spaghetti

3 cups broccoli slaw or kale slaw mix (see Kitchen Whizdom)

½ English cucumber, sliced into thin ribbons

1 medium red bell pepper, thinly sliced

½ cup frozen shelled edamame, thawed

½ cup chopped green onions

½ cup chopped roasted salted peanuts

⅓ to ½ cup chopped fresh cilantro

Whisk together all dressing ingredients in a small bowl until well blended or whirl in a small blender for dressing that's extra creamy and emulsified. Set aside.

Cook spaghetti according to package directions. Drain, rinse with cold water (to stop the cooking action) and drain again. Transfer spaghetti to a large bowl.

Add remaining salad ingredients to cooked spaghetti and mix well. Add the dressing and mix again, until ingredients are well coated. You can dig right in or store the salad in the fridge for a couple of hours before serving.

Makes 6 servings

Per serving: 348 calories, 14.8 g total fat (2.1 g saturated fat), 11 g protein, 45 g carbohydrate (3.8 g fiber, 7.4 g sugars), 0 mg cholesterol, 309 mg sodium

For convenience, I buy the smallest bag of slaw mix like broccoli slaw or kale slaw and toss it in this salad. About 3 cups slaw mix is the right amount. The combo of red and green cabbage, carrots, grated broccoli and/or chopped kale works well in this salad to add texture, color and crunch.

SWAP IT
Green peas can be used instead of edamame.
Try it with quinoa spaghetti
TOP IT
Garnish with more chopped peanuts and cilantro or green onions.

Pasta

Dill-icious Crabmeat Pasta Salad

with shell pasta and dreamy, creamy dressing

This crabsolutely fabulous pasta salad is a simple yet scrumptious summer barbecue staple. Don't be afraid to use imitation crabmeat, since the price of real crabmeat can be ridiculously expensive.

Dressing

½ cup mayonnaise (light or regular)

½ cup plain 0% Greek yogurt or light (5%) sour cream

1 tbsp white wine vinegar

1 tbsp freshly squeezed lemon juice

1 tbsp minced fresh dill

1 tsp yellow mustard

½ tsp celery seed

¼ tsp sea salt

⅛ tsp freshly ground black pepper

Salad

12 oz (340 g) uncooked medium shell pasta

1 lb (454 g) lump crabmeat (real or imitation)

½ cup each diced red and green bell peppers

½ cup diced celery

½ cup chopped green onions

Whisk together all dressing ingredients in a small bowl. Cover and refrigerate until ready to use.

Cook pasta shells according to package directions. Drain, rinse with cold water (to stop the cooking action) and drain again. Transfer cooked shells to a large bowl.

Add remaining salad ingredients to pasta and mix well. Add the prepared dressing and mix again, until all ingredients are well coated. Cover and refrigerate until chilled, about 2 hours. Top with a few grinds of black pepper before serving.

Makes about 8 cups salad

Per cup: 237 calories, 5.2 g total fat (0.5 g saturated fat), 14.5 g protein, 35 g carbohydrate (3.1 g fiber, 2.5 g sugars), 62 mg cholesterol, 423 mg sodium

If possible, make the dressing in advance and let it sit in the fridge for a few hours or overnight before adding it to the salad. It's my humble, unscientific opinion that homemade, creamy dressings benefit from chilling and intermingling of ingredients versus vinaigrettes, which are super-tasty the second they're made.

SWITCH IT UP
Use chopped, cooked shrimp instead of crabmeat.
JAZZ IT UP
Add ¾ cup thawed, frozen green peas.
Use REAL or imitation crabmeat.

Noodle KNOW-HOW:

Secrets to perfectly cooked pasta for standout salads

1. PICK THE RIGHT PASTA.

The more nooks, crannies and curves, the better your pasta will hold the dressing. Since plump rotini has more twists than a bad soap opera, it's my top choice for salads. Second place: penne rigate (with ridges). Third place: farfalle (bow ties).

2. SALT IT LIKE YOU MEAN IT.

Pasta itself is pretty bland, so salting the cooking water is essential. Think of it as seasoning from the inside out. Add 1 tablespoon salt per gallon (4 L) of cooking water.

3. COOK LIKE GOLDILOCKS.

Aim for just right! This means taking pasta one step *past* al dente. (Cue the eye roll from the Italians!) But pasta firms up as it cools, so if your pasta starts out with some chew/bite, it'll taste undercooked after being refrigerated.

4. COOL IT DOWN.

Rinse the cooked, drained pasta under cold water to stop the cooking action and prevent clumping. This applies only to cooking pasta for cold salads, but not for hot entrées. Optional: Toss rinsed noodles with a splash of olive oil while they wait to join the pasta salad party.

Pasta

Chicken BLT Pasta Salad

with creamy poppy seed dressing

This crowd-pleasing salad has Father's Day BBQ, long-weekend cookout or summer potluck party written all over it! Chicken. Pasta. Bacon. Creamy dressing. Need I say more? Yup, it's wickedly delicious and worth the splurge.

Dressing

½ cup mayonnaise (light or regular)

½ cup plain 0% Greek yogurt

1½ tbsp white wine vinegar

1 tbsp freshly squeezed lemon juice

1 tbsp granulated sugar or liquid honey

2 tsp poppy seeds

½ tsp mustard powder

¼ tsp sea salt

⅛ tsp freshly ground black pepper

Salad

1 pkg (13 oz/375 g) uncooked rotini

2 cups chopped romaine hearts or chopped baby spinach

2 cups chopped cooked chicken breast

1 cup halved or quartered grape tomatoes

8 slices bacon, cooked and chopped

¾ cup frozen green peas, thawed

½ cup chopped green onions

Freshly ground black pepper to taste

Whisk together all dressing ingredients in a small bowl or measuring cup. Cover and refrigerate until ready to use.

Cook rotini according to package directions. Drain, rinse with cold water (to stop the cooking action) and drain again. Transfer rotini to a very large bowl.

Add remaining salad ingredients to cooked rotini and mix well. Add the prepared dressing and mix again, until all ingredients are well coated. Serve immediately. See Kitchen Whizdom for make-ahead tips.

Makes about 10 cups salad

Per cup: 306 calories, 12.3 g total fat (2 g saturated fat), 16.5 g protein, 30.6 g carbohydrate (4.4 g fiber, 3.6 g sugars), 76 mg cholesterol, 255 mg sodium

If preparing this salad in advance, add the dressing and greens (romaine or spinach) just before serving. Otherwise, the noodles will soak up all the dressing and the greens will be wilty and wimpy. You don't want that! I prefer the fat, plump rotini noodles in this salad versus the skinny, no personality, rotini-wannabe fusilli. Rotini was perfectly designed by the Italians to hold sauces and dressings better than most pasta shapes.

SWAP IT
Not crazy about poppy seed dressing? Use ranch or Caesar dressing instead.
TOP IT
A bit of shredded sharp cheddar makes it even *beddar!*
LOADED with FLAVOR

Pasta

Grilled Vegetable Pasta Salad

with bow-tie pasta, colorful veggies, fresh basil and feta

It's a bow-tie bow-nanza! For the grill seeker in you, here's a flavor-packed, summertime recipe to get fired up about. This mouthwatering pasta salad is loaded with grilled vegetables and tastes great served warm or chilled.

Dressing

3 tbsp olive oil

3 tbsp balsamic vinegar

3 tbsp freshly squeezed lemon juice

2 tbsp pure maple syrup

1 tbsp Dijon mustard

1 tsp minced garlic

¼ tsp sea salt

⅛ tsp freshly ground black pepper

Salad

1 medium red bell pepper, cut into 1-inch pieces

1 medium yellow bell pepper, cut into 1-inch pieces

1 medium yellow zucchini, cut into ½-inch-thick rounds

1 medium green zucchini, cut into ½-inch-thick rounds

1 medium red onion, cut into 6 wedges

1 pkg (8 oz/227 g) whole cremini mushrooms or mini portobello mushrooms, coarsely chopped

1 pkg (13 oz/375 g) uncooked farfalle (bow-tie) pasta

⅓ cup chopped fresh basil

1 cup crumbled light or regular feta cheese (4 oz/113 g)

Note: You'll need two grill baskets to make this recipe.

Make the dressing: Whisk together all dressing ingredients in a small bowl or measuring cup. Cover and refrigerate until ready to use.

Preheat grill to high heat. Spray two grill baskets with cooking spray or lightly brush with olive oil. Add chopped vegetables and mix well. Place baskets on grill racks, reduce heat to medium and close lid. Cook vegetables for about 20 minutes, stirring occasionally, until tender with nice grill marks.

Meanwhile, cook pasta according to package directions. Drain and keep warm. (Don't forget about the vegetables on the grill!)

Add grilled vegetables and cooked pasta to a very large bowl and mix well. Give the prepared dressing a good whisk and add it to the salad, along with basil and feta. Mix again. Top with freshly ground black pepper, if desired. Serve immediately.

Makes about 10 cups salad

Per cup: 242 calories, 6.5 g total fat (1.8 g saturated fat), 10 g protein, 37 g carbohydrate (2 g fiber, 7.8 g sugars), 5.6 mg cholesterol, 239 mg sodium

When asparagus is in season, it's a delicious addition to this salad. Serve the salad alone as a vegetarian meal or alongside just about anything grilled: chicken breasts or thighs, salmon, steak or burgers. A non-stick grill basket is a handy, inexpensive piece of cookware that you'll use again and again. Look for grill baskets wherever barbecues and grilling tools are sold.

SWAP IT

I love this salad made with whole wheat rotini. Try it!

TOP IT

Take the dressing over the top by adding 2 tbsp mayonnaise for a bit of creamy richness.

Loaded Italian Pasta Salad*

with salami, fresh mozzarella and Parmesan dressing

This impressive, boldly flavored salad is the perfect pick to feed a crowd! Plus, with meat, cheese, veggies and a zippy dressing, it's substantial enough to serve for supper. Buon appetito!

**No drunk Italians were involved in the creation of this recipe. It's the salad that's loaded. My Italian editor forced me to clarify this.* ☺

Salad

1 pkg (13 oz/375 g) uncooked rotini (regular or whole wheat)

1 tub (7 oz/200 g) mini bocconcini (fresh mozzarella), drained

6 oz (170 g) salami (spicy or mild), chopped (see Kitchen Whizdom)

1½ cups halved cherry or grape tomatoes

¾ cup chopped roasted red peppers (from a jar)

½ cup thinly sliced red onions

½ cup sliced Kalamata olives

½ cup chopped fresh parsley

Dressing

½ cup olive oil

¼ cup red wine vinegar

3 tbsp finely grated Parmesan cheese

2 tbsp freshly squeezed lemon juice

1 tbsp liquid honey

1 tsp minced garlic

1 tsp Dijon mustard

½ tsp each dried oregano and dried basil

¼ tsp each sea salt and freshly ground black pepper

Cook rotini according to package directions. Drain, rinse with cold water (to stop the cooking action) and drain again. Transfer rotini to a very large bowl.

Add bocconcini, salami, tomatoes, roasted peppers, onions, olives and parsley. Mix well.

Whisk together all dressing ingredients in a small bowl or measuring cup. Alternatively, whirl ingredients in a small blender or shake them up in a jar. Pour dressing over salad and mix until all salad ingredients are well coated.

Refrigerate for at least 6 hours before serving for the best flavor. The ingredients need time to mingle! Leftovers will keep for 2 to 3 days in a sealed container in the fridge.

Makes about 10 cups salad

Per cup: 385 calories, 21.7 g total fat (6.3 g saturated fat), 16 g protein, 32 g carbohydrate (3.5 g fiber, 4 g sugars), 30 mg cholesterol, 397 mg sodium

Not a fan of salami? No problem! Use chopped pepperoni, ham, chicken breast or kielbasa (I like turkey kielbasa!) instead. For a meatless version, skip the salami and throw in a small can of drained and rinsed chickpeas. Fresh basil in your garden? Toss in a bit of that, too.

Wickedly Delicious
Splurge-Worthy
Totally worth it!
SWAP IT
Try gluten-free rotini instead of wheat-based pasta.
TOP IT
Add some freshly grated Parmesan right before serving.

Mexican Street Corn Pasta Salad

with charred corn and smoky lime dressing

I've always loved corn, especially when grilled or charred in a skillet. Add some cute little pasta tubes, a creamy lime dressing with a hint of smoked paprika (think barbecue chips!), throw in some fresh cilantro and watch me totally lose my mind and all self-control! Take this to your next gathering and expect rave reviews and requests for the recipe.

Dressing

½ cup light mayonnaise

⅓ cup 14% (full-fat) sour cream

2 tbsp freshly squeezed lime juice

1 tbsp liquid honey

1 tsp grated lime zest

½ tsp smoked paprika

¼ tsp ground cumin

1 tsp Sriracha hot sauce (optional)

Salad

8 oz (227 g) uncooked ditali pasta (4 cups cooked; see Kitchen Whizdom)

8 medium cobs fresh corn, shucked

1 tbsp olive oil

1 cup diced red bell peppers

1 cup grated Cotija cheese (see Kitchen Whizdom)

½ cup chopped green onions

⅓ cup minced fresh cilantro

1 jalapeño pepper, seeded and minced

Sea salt and freshly ground black pepper to taste

Whisk together all dressing ingredients in a small bowl. Cover and refrigerate until ready to use.

Cook pasta according to package directions. Drain, rinse with cold water (to stop the cooking action) and drain again. Transfer cooked pasta to a large bowl and set aside.

Preheat grill to medium-high heat. Brush corn lightly with olive oil. Place cobs directly on the grill. Close lid and grill corn until char marks appear and corn is tender, rotating cobs every 2 to 3 minutes. Total cooking time will be 10 to 12 minutes. Remove corn from heat.

When corn is cool enough to handle, slice the kernels off the cob and add to pasta, along with all remaining salad ingredients. Mix well. Add the dressing and mix again, until ingredients are well coated. Season with a pinch of salt and pepper, if desired. Chill for 2 hours before serving.

Makes about 10 cups salad

Per cup: 259 calories, 9.1 g total fat (2.4 g saturated fat), 8.3 g protein, 36 g carbohydrate (3.4 g fiber, 6.3 g sugars), 8 mg cholesterol, 225 mg sodium

Ditali is small, tube-shaped pasta that's most often used in soups—not to be confused with ditalini, also tube-shaped and often used in soups. LOL! Ditalini is tiny. You want small ditali. Regarding the salty, crumbly, delicious Mexican Cotija (cō-TEE-ha) cheese, it's becoming more popular, and I found it at my regular grocery store near the specialty cheeses.

SWAP IT
Use 3/4 cup finely crumbled light feta cheese instead of the Cotija.
¡ESTÁ delicioso!
TOP IT
Love avocados? Add 1 diced avocado just before serving.

Pasta

Primavera Pesto Pasta Salad

with tri-color rotini and pesto vinaigrette

*

"Eating the rainbow" has never been easier, thanks to this veggie-loaded, lick-your-lips delicious salad featuring asparagus, broccoli, peas, cherry tomatoes and crunchy bell peppers. Meal prep it for lunches or take it to a party and watch it disappear!

Dressing

½ cup olive oil

¼ cup red wine vinegar

3 tbsp basil pesto (see Kitchen Whizdom)

1 tbsp freshly squeezed lemon juice

2 tsp liquid honey

1 tsp Dijon mustard

½ tsp grated lemon zest

¼ tsp freshly ground black pepper

Salad

1 lb (454 g) uncooked tri-color rotini*

2 cups small broccoli florets

2 cups chopped fresh asparagus

1½ cups halved cherry tomatoes

¾ cup fresh green peas (thaw first if using frozen)

¾ cup each diced or sliced red and yellow bell peppers

½ cup freshly grated Parmesan cheese or ¾ cup crumbled feta cheese

½ cup chopped fresh parsley

*For gluten-free, use GF rotini or fusilli.

Whisk together all dressing ingredients in a small bowl or whirl them in a small blender until well mixed. Refrigerate until ready to use.

Cook rotini according to package directions. During the last minute of cooking time, add broccoli and asparagus and blanch for 1 minute. Notice the bright green color? Yay! Drain pasta and veggies, rinse with cold water (to stop the cooking action) and drain again. Transfer mixture to a very large bowl.

Add remaining salad ingredients and mix well. Add the dressing and mix again, until all ingredients are well coated. Refrigerate for at least 4 hours for flavors to develop. Add a few grinds of freshly ground black pepper before serving.

Makes about 14 cups salad

Per cup: 241 calories, 10.8 g total fat (2.2 g saturated fat), 7.5 g protein, 29.7 g carbohydrate (2.8 g fiber, 3.5 g sugars), 4 mg cholesterol, 112 mg sodium.

Homemade basil pesto is the besto, but if you prefer the convenience of store-bought pesto (or it's the dead of winter and fresh basil has disappeared from your garden), search for a brand that uses extra-virgin olive oil, not the cheaper soybean or canola oils, which have a completely different flavor. Freeze extra pesto in ice cube trays, then store the frozen pesto cubes in a resealable freezer bag.

SWAP IT

Try bow-tie pasta instead of rotini. Look for bow ties with ridges—the dressing clings better.

TOP IT

Garnish with more freshly grated Parmesan or feta; Kalamata olives are a tasty addition!

Pasta

Tortellini & Chickpea Salad

with fresh veggies, herbs and Italian dressing

May I offer a tidbit of advice? Don't wait for a potluck invite to get some pasta salad magic in your life! I could live on this salad for days (and I have!). It's vegetarian, but you can add whatever meat your protein-loving heart desires.

Dressing

½ cup olive oil

¼ cup red wine vinegar

3 tbsp finely grated Parmesan cheese

2 tbsp freshly squeezed lemon juice

1 tbsp liquid honey

1 tsp minced garlic

1 tsp Dijon mustard

½ tsp each dried oregano and dried basil

¼ tsp each sea salt and freshly ground black pepper

Salad

1 lb (454 g) uncooked cheese tortellini*

1 can (19 oz/540 mL) no-salt-added chickpeas, drained and rinsed

1½ cups diced English cucumbers

1½ cups halved cherry tomatoes

1 small handful baby arugula or baby spinach

½ cup very thinly sliced red onions

½ cup chopped fresh flat-leaf parsley

2 tbsp chopped fresh basil or minced fresh dill

Freshly grated Parmesan for serving (optional)

***Use fresh, refrigerated tortellini.**

Whisk together all dressing ingredients in a small bowl or measuring cup. Alternatively, whirl them in a small blender for an extra-smooth dressing. Refrigerate until ready to use.

Cook tortellini according to package directions. Be careful not to overcook it. Drain, rinse with cold water (to stop the cooking action) and drain again. Transfer tortellini to a large bowl.

Add all remaining salad ingredients (except Parmesan, if using) to tortellini. Mix well. Add dressing and mix again, until all ingredients are well coated. Cover and refrigerate until chilled, about 2 hours. Serve with extra grated Parmesan, if desired, and a few grinds of black pepper.

Makes about 10 cups salad

Per cup: 345 calories, 15 g total fat (2.8 g saturated fat), 11 g protein, 42 g carbohydrate (3.9 g fiber, 5 g sugars), 21 mg cholesterol, 344 mg sodium

SWAP IT

For convenience, use your favorite store-bought Italian dressing and add the optional fresh Parmesan.

TOP IT

A bit of chopped salami or pepperoni never hurt anyone. ☺

Pasta

Tasty Tuna Noodle Salad

with crunchy veggies and chopped pickles

*

Pickle lovers unite! This delicious tuna pasta salad not only contains chopped dill pickles, but also includes some dill pickle juice, which permeates and elevates the creamy dressing with its irresistible briny tang.

Dressing

½ cup 0% plain Greek yogurt

½ cup mayonnaise (light or regular)

¼ cup dill pickle juice

1½ tbsp honey mustard

1 tbsp minced fresh dill

1 tsp grated lemon zest

⅛ tsp freshly ground black pepper

Salad

10 oz (285 g) uncooked fusilli or rotini*

3 cans (6 oz/170 g each) tuna, drained (see Kitchen Whizdom)

1 cup finely chopped red bell peppers

1 cup chopped dill pickles

¾ cup finely chopped celery

½ cup minced red onions

3 tbsp minced fresh parsley

Freshly ground black pepper and sea salt to taste

***For gluten-free, use a GF pasta made from brown rice, quinoa, chickpeas or lentils.**

Whisk together all dressing ingredients in a small bowl. Cover and refrigerate until ready to use.

Cook pasta according to package directions. Drain, rinse with cold water (to stop the cooking action) and drain again. Transfer pasta to a large bowl.

Add remaining salad ingredients to cooked pasta and mix well. Add the dressing and mix again, until all ingredients are well coated. Add a bit more freshly ground pepper and a pinch of sea salt, if desired. Serve immediately or chill slightly before serving. (The longer it chills, the less creamy the salad becomes, since the pasta soaks up the dressing. It never hurts to make extra dressing to refresh leftover pasta salads!)

Makes about 12 cups salad

Per cup: 163 calories, 3.5 g total fat (0.4 g saturated fat), 12.1 g protein, 20.5 g carbohydrate (2.3 g fiber, 2 g sugars), 15 mg cholesterol, 261 mg sodium

I prefer using water-packed albacore tuna for this recipe, however, it can be expensive. (What isn't expensive these days?!) Make a habit of scanning the canned tuna and salmon aisle and stocking up when items are on sale. For a special treat and an incredible flavor boost, buy six little cans (3 oz/85 g each) of Clover Leaf Dill & Lemon tuna and use them in this salad. DILLectable! (Bonus: They're often on sale.)

PASTA FOR PICKLE PEOPLE

JAZZ IT UP

Toss in ½ cup thawed, frozen green peas.

SWITCH IT UP

Swap the red onions for chopped green onions and use medium shell pasta instead of fusilli/rotini.

Easy Peasy Orzo Salad

with green peas, chickpeas and fresh mint

It's easy, it's peasy, it's feta cheesy! Fresh and flavorful, this pretty (and pretty filling!) salad can be made in advance, so it's a perfect pick for potlucks, parties or to pack for lunch.

Salad

2 cups uncooked orzo (rice-shaped pasta)

1 cup quartered grape tomatoes

1 cup peeled, diced English cucumbers

1 cup canned no-salt-added chickpeas, drained and rinsed

1 cup crumbled light or regular feta cheese (4 oz/113 g)

¾ cup fresh or frozen green peas (thaw first if using frozen; see Kitchen Whizdom)

½ cup chopped green onions

¼ cup chopped fresh mint

Dressing

⅓ cup olive oil

3 tbsp red wine vinegar

1 tbsp freshly squeezed lemon juice

1 tbsp liquid honey

1 tsp minced garlic

½ tsp Dijon mustard

¼ tsp each sea salt and freshly ground black pepper

Cook orzo according to package directions. Drain, rinse with cold water (to stop the cooking action) and drain again.

In a large bowl, combine cooked orzo and all remaining salad ingredients. Stir gently.

Whisk together all dressing ingredients in a small bowl or measuring cup. Pour over salad and stir until ingredients are well coated. Cover and refrigerate for at least 4 hours before serving for the best flavor.

Makes about 8 cups salad

Per cup: 324 calories, 12.6 g total fat (3 g saturated fat), 11.7 g protein, 42 g carbohydrate (4.8 g fiber, 5.4 g sugars), 7 mg cholesterol, 269 mg sodium

There's no need to cook fresh or frozen peas before using them in this salad. However, a simple trick I use to thaw and "refresh" frozen peas is to place them in a colander/strainer in the sink, then pour the orzo with its hot cooking water over top. Drain well, then rinse with cold water (as directed in the recipe) and drain again. Your pretty peas and pasta are good to go!

SWAP IT

Instead of fresh mint and feta, try dill and Parmesan, but cut quantities in half.

TOP IT

Sprinkle with 1/3 cup sliced almonds before serving to add some crunch.

CHAPTER 4

THE BEAN SCENE

Beautiful, bountiful salads featuring chickpeas, beans and lentils.

RED KIDNEY BEANS

13.4 g protein

16.3 g fiber

NAVY BEANS

14.9 g protein

19.1 g fiber

Sometimes it's good to be...

BROWN LENTILS*

17.9 g protein

15.6 g fiber

PINTO BEANS

15.4 g protein

15.3 g fiber

*Lentils and beans are both types of legumes. Lentils aren't technically beans, but they belong to the same family.

BLACK BEANS

15.2 g protein

14.9 g fiber

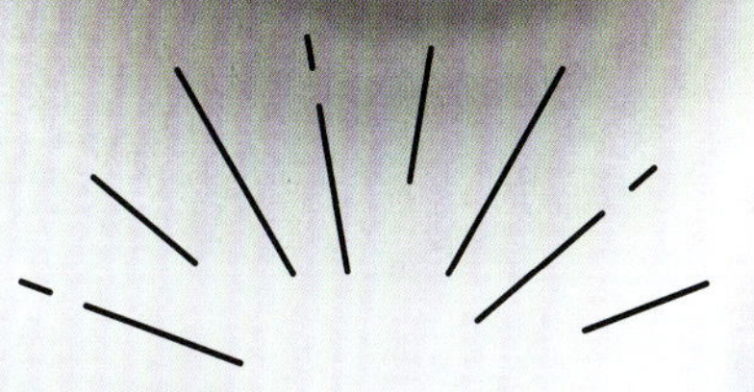

CHICKPEAS

14.5 g protein

12.5 g fiber

FULL of BEANS

BLACK-EYED PEAS

13 g protein

11 g fiber

WHITE KIDNEY BEANS (CANNELLINI)

17 g protein

11 g fiber

Per 1-cup cooked beans

Lentil & Black Bean Salad

with chopped veggies and fresh parsley

Make it once, eat it all week! Everyone loves this simple, staple salad recipe featuring pantry staples: lentils, black beans and corn. It's crisp, colorful, crunchy and crave-worthy!

Salad

1 can (19 oz/540 mL) lentils, drained and rinsed

1 can (19 oz/540 mL) no-salt-added black beans, drained and rinsed

1 can (12 oz/340 mL) whole-kernel corn, drained

1 cup diced red bell peppers

¾ cup each diced celery and diced green bell peppers

½ cup chopped green onions

¼ cup chopped fresh parsley

Dressing

¼ cup olive oil or good-quality vegetable oil

3 tbsp red wine vinegar

1 tbsp freshly squeezed lemon juice

1 tbsp liquid honey (use pure maple syrup for vegan)

½ tsp Dijon mustard

¼ tsp each sea salt and freshly ground black pepper

Combine all salad ingredients in a large bowl. Set aside.

Whisk together all dressing ingredients in a small bowl or measuring cup. Pour over salad and mix well. Be careful not to squish the lentils and beans. Taste and adjust for salt and pepper, if desired. Refrigerate for at least 4 hours before serving. (Tastes even better if made 1 day ahead. I know, that's a long time to wait!)

Makes about 10 cups salad

Per cup: 186 calories, 6.6 g total fat (0.9 g saturated fat), 8 g protein, 26 g carbohydrate (7 g fiber, 4 g sugars), 0 mg cholesterol, 154 mg sodium

Look for no-salt-added beans to keep the sodium count low. If you can't find the reduced-sodium variety, make sure you drain and rinse the beans well. I often use organic sunflower or safflower oil in this recipe and others that benefit from a neutral-tasting oil.

SWAP IT

Try white balsamic vinegar instead of red wine vinegar.

TOP IT

Drained canned tuna adds even more protein!

Chickpea, Tomato & Bocconcini Salad

with fresh basil and balsamic dressing

Tomatoes and basil are a match made in culinary heaven. Add some fresh mozzarella, hearty chickpeas and a simple balsamic dressing, then watch this salad get devoured as quickly as it was made!

Salad

1 can (19 oz/540 mL) no-salt-added chickpeas, drained and rinsed

2 cups halved cherry tomatoes

1 tub (7 oz/200 g) mini bocconcini (fresh mozzarella), drained

⅓ cup thinly sliced or minced red onions

⅓ cup chopped fresh basil (see Kitchen Whizdom)

Dressing

2 tbsp olive oil

2 tbsp balsamic vinegar

2 tsp liquid honey or pure maple syrup

½ tsp Dijon mustard

¼ tsp each sea salt and freshly ground black pepper

Combine all salad ingredients in a large bowl and mix well. Set aside.

Whisk together all dressing ingredients in a small bowl or measuring cup. Pour over salad and mix gently until all ingredients are well coated with dressing. Add a few more grinds of black pepper and serve immediately.

Makes about 5 cups salad

Per cup: 282 calories, 15 g total fat (5.7 g saturated fat), 14 g protein, 22.8 g carbohydrate (4.4 g fiber, 5.6 g sugars), 27 mg cholesterol, 133 mg sodium

Fresh basil MAKES this recipe, so please don't leave it out or use dried basil. Every summer, I grow my own basil and dream up ways to use it. This salad is on repeat at my house for this very reason. Oh, and the fact that it's delicious and I can throw it together in 10 minutes. I've successfully made this salad in the winter (cravings are cravings!) by using super-tasty Campari tomatoes and 2 tablespoons basil pesto instead of the fresh herb. Either way, it's bursting with basiliciousness.

SWAP IT
Use 1 cup cubed feta cheese instead of mozzarella.
TOP IT
Add a medium diced avocado just before serving.

Black-Eyed Pea Salad

with colorful diced veggies and balsamic dressing

Tempt your taste buds with this gorgeous, vibrant salad bursting with veggie and bean goodness! It's deliciously crisp and fresh, plus it lasts for days in the fridge. Except it won't last for days in the fridge, if you know what I mean. And the tasty balsamic dressing is the icing on the cake! Except it isn't the icing on the cake. (OK, fine, I'll stop—you have a salad to make.)

Salad

2 cans (19 oz/540 mL each) black-eyed peas, drained and rinsed

1½ cups quartered grape or cherry tomatoes

1 cup diced English cucumbers

1 cup diced celery

1 cup diced orange or yellow bell peppers

½ cup chopped fresh parsley

½ cup finely chopped red onions

Dressing

¼ cup olive oil

3 tbsp balsamic vinegar

1 tbsp freshly squeezed lemon juice

1 tbsp pure maple syrup

1 tsp Dijon mustard

1 tsp minced garlic

¼ tsp each sea salt and freshly ground black pepper

Combine all salad ingredients in a large bowl and mix well. Set aside.

Make the dressing: Whisk together all dressing ingredients in a small bowl or measuring cup. (Alternatively, you can shake them up in a mason jar or whirl them in a small blender.)

Pour dressing over salad and mix gently until all ingredients are well coated. Add a few more grinds of black pepper and serve immediately or cover and refrigerate for a couple hours (or up to 1 day) before serving. I prefer this salad at room temperature.

Makes about 9 cups salad

Per cup: 164 calories, 6.7 g total fat (0.9 g saturated fat), 6.7 g protein, 21.6 g carbohydrate (4.2 g fiber, 4.7 g sugars), 0 mg cholesterol, 161 mg sodium

Black-eyed peas aren't actually peas—they're beans, and they get their name from their appearance. That little black speck, resembling an eye in the center of the beans, marks the spot where they were once attached to pods. You'll find them in canned and dried versions at any well-stocked grocery store. Chickpeas or lentils are both excellent substitutes for the black-eyed peas in this recipe.

SWITCH IT UP
Use cilantro and lime juice instead of parsley and lemon juice.
JAZZ IT UP
Add 1 cup grilled or skillet-charred corn.

TEX-MEX

Black Bean & Corn Salad

with mangoes and avocados

DF

Though this colorful salad looks and tastes like summer, you'll enjoy it all year round as a delicious, filling, vegetarian lunch or a wildly popular side dish for family gatherings. I'd rank it in my Top 10 favorite salad recipes of all time and I'm certain I can make it with my eyes closed. (Do not attempt this at home.)

Salad

1 can (19 oz/540 mL) no-salt-added black beans, drained and rinsed

1 can (12 oz/340 mL) whole-kernel corn, drained

1 large mango, peeled and diced

1 cup quartered grape tomatoes

1 cup diced red bell peppers

½ cup chopped green onions

¼ cup minced fresh cilantro

1 small jalapeño pepper, seeded and minced

Dressing

2 tbsp freshly squeezed lime juice

1 tbsp olive oil

¼ tsp each ground cumin and chili powder

¼ tsp each sea salt and freshly ground black pepper

1 large avocado, diced

Combine all salad ingredients in a large bowl and mix well.

Add lime juice, olive oil, cumin, chili powder, salt and pepper and stir until all ingredients are coated with seasonings. Gently stir in the avocado and serve immediately.

Makes about 8 cups salad

Per cup: 124 calories, 4.8 g total fat (0.6 g saturated fat), 4.5 g protein, 19 g carbohydrate (6.1 g fiber, 6.8 g sugars), 0 mg cholesterol, 119 mg sodium

After adding the dressing, taste the salad and adjust the spices according to your taste buds. Want it spicier? Add a pinch of cayenne pepper and double the cumin and chili powder. Needs a bit more salt and pepper? Go for it! You can make this salad a day in advance, but since avocados turn brown quickly, it's best to stir them in just before serving.

One of my
MOST POPULAR
salad recipes!
SWITCH IT UP
Use smoked paprika instead
of chili powder.
JAZZ IT UP
Add some grilled shrimp or
chicken for a tasty protein boost.

Beans

LIGHT & LEMONY

Chickpea & Kidney Bean Salad

with crunchy cucumbers and fresh herbs

GF DF V

Sometimes less is more and simple can be scrumptious—which is certainly true when it comes to this fresh-tasting, healthy, throw-it-together-in-minutes vegan bean salad. It's not fancy, but it's fantastic! Bonus: It lasts for days in the fridge and tastes even better the longer the beans marinate in the dressing.

Salad

1 can (19 oz/540 mL) no-salt-added chickpeas, drained and rinsed

1 can (19 oz/540 mL) no-salt-added red kidney beans, drained and rinsed

1½ cups diced English cucumbers

1 cup diced celery

½ cup thinly sliced red onions

½ cup chopped fresh parsley

3 tbsp minced fresh dill

Dressing

¼ cup olive oil

2 tbsp freshly squeezed lemon juice

2 tbsp apple cider vinegar or red wine vinegar

1 tbsp pure maple syrup

2 tsp Dijon mustard

1 tsp minced garlic

1 tsp grated lemon zest

½ tsp sea salt

¼ tsp freshly ground black pepper

Combine all salad ingredients in a large bowl and mix well.

Make the dressing: Whisk together all dressing ingredients in a small bowl or measuring cup. Pour over salad and stir gently. Cover and refrigerate for at least 2 hours before serving.

Makes about 8 cups salad

Per cup: 190 calories, 8.2 g total fat (1.1 g saturated fat), 7.6 g protein, 23.7 g carbohydrate (6.2 g fiber, 3.1 g sugars), 0 mg cholesterol, 119 mg sodium

When recipes call for both lemon juice and grated zest, don't forget to zest the lemon before you juice it! Once squeezed, it's kinda tricky to zest a lemon. In "proper" recipe writing and formatting, ingredients are listed in order of use and in descending quantities. When making salad dressings, all ingredients are whisked together in one step, which means lemon juice gets listed before lemon zest, since the juice quantity is always larger. Feel free to dazzle your friends with this life-altering information at your next social gathering.

SWAP IT
Not keen about kidney beans?
Use navy beans instead.
TOP IT
Tastes great with some
crumbled or cubed feta cheese.

Chopped Cauliflower & Chickpea Salad

with maple-curry vinaigrette

Though it might seem like an odd combination of ingredients, I love this flavorful, crunchy salad, modeled after one I tasted years ago while on vacation. It benefits from "marinating" time in the fridge, so make it at least a couple hours before you plan to eat it.

Salad

3 cups finely chopped cauliflower florets

1 can (19 oz/540 mL) no-salt-added chickpeas, drained and rinsed

¾ cup grated carrots

¾ cup frozen green peas, thawed (see Kitchen Whizdom)

½ cup chopped green onions

⅓ cup chopped raisins or dates

¼ cup minced fresh cilantro

Dressing

⅓ cup light-tasting olive oil

¼ cup apple cider vinegar

2 tbsp pure maple syrup

1½ tbsp Dijon mustard

2 tsp curry powder (mild, medium or hot)

½ tsp ground cumin

¼ tsp each sea salt and freshly ground black pepper

Combine all salad ingredients in a large bowl and mix well. Set aside.

Make the dressing: Whisk together all dressing ingredients in a small bowl or measuring cup.

Pour dressing over salad and mix gently until all ingredients are well coated. Add a few more grinds of black pepper, cover and refrigerate for 2 hours (or up to 1 day) before serving.

FYI: Green peas will start to lose their vibrant color the longer the salad is stored in the fridge.

Makes about 7 cups salad

Per cup: 230 calories, 11.9 g total fat (1.7 g saturated fat), 6 g protein, 27 g carbohydrate (5.2 g fiber, 10.5 g sugars), 0 mg cholesterol, 212 mg sodium

Fresh peas—beautifully green and perfectly round—would be lovely in this salad, however, they aren't always available. That's why I suggest dependable and delicious frozen peas as an option. Picked at the peak of ripeness and flash frozen, meaning they've retained most of their nutrients, I'm officially declaring myself Captain of Team Frozen. Just place the frozen peas in a mesh sieve and run them under warm water until they're thawed. No cooking is required for use in a salad.

SWAP IT
Use dried currants instead of raisins or dates.
TOP IT
Sprinkle with 1/4 cup chopped or sliced almonds before serving.

Beans

Sunflower Crunch Edamame Salad

with a sweet-and-savory sesame-ginger dressing

Trust me, this is not a tasteless pile of soybeans! It's a showstopping edamame and lentil salad that's bright, beautiful and brimming with flavor, thanks to the Asian-inspired dressing and the colorful mix of vibrant veggies. Toss in some crunchy sunflower seeds and fresh cilantro and try not to eat the whole bowlful!

Salad

1 can (19 oz/540 mL) lentils, drained and rinsed

2 cups frozen shelled edamame, thawed

1½ cups diced English cucumbers (peeled or unpeeled)

1 cup grated red cabbage

1 cup grated carrots

1 cup diced red bell peppers

½ cup chopped green onions

½ cup roasted salted sunflower seeds

⅓ cup chopped fresh cilantro

Dressing

⅓ cup hoisin sauce

2 tbsp sunflower oil or peanut oil

2 tbsp dark sesame oil

2 tbsp freshly squeezed lime juice

2 tbsp seasoned rice vinegar

1 tbsp grated fresh gingerroot

1 tsp minced garlic

1 tsp grated lime zest

Pinch crushed red pepper flakes

***For gluten-free, use GF hoisin sauce. The popular Lee Kum Kee brand makes a GF version.**

Combine all salad ingredients in a large bowl and mix well. Set aside.

Make the dressing: Whisk together all dressing ingredients in a small bowl or measuring cup. (Alternatively, you can shake them up in a mason jar or whirl them in a small blender.)

Pour dressing over salad and mix gently until all ingredients are well coated. Tongs work well for this purpose. May be served immediately or covered and stored in the fridge for up to 1 day before serving.

Makes about 9 cups salad

Per cup: 213 calories, 11.6 g total fat (1.2 g saturated fat), 8.5 g protein, 20 g carbohydrate (4.9 g fiber, 8.4 g sugars), 0 mg cholesterol, 315 mg sodium

SWITCH IT UP

Trade the sunflower seeds for sliced almonds or chopped peanuts.

JAZZ IT UP

Add 1 tbsp sunflower butter or peanut butter to the dressing.

Lentil & Toasted Pine Nut Salad

with dried cranberries and apple cider vinaigrette

DF

As humble as lentils are, they're super versatile and so tasty when paired with fresh herbs and delectable dressings. May I present to you Exhibit A: a light and lovely autumn-like lentil salad you can make in minutes and eat for days!

Dressing

3 tbsp olive oil

3 tbsp apple cider vinegar

1 tbsp freshly squeezed lemon juice

1 tbsp pure maple syrup

1 tsp Dijon mustard

1 tsp minced garlic

¼ tsp sea salt

⅛ tsp freshly ground black pepper

Salad

2 cans (19 oz/540 mL each) lentils, drained and rinsed

1½ cups finely chopped English cucumbers (see Kitchen Whizdom)

¾ cup sweetened dried cranberries, chopped

½ cup minced red onions

½ cup toasted pine nuts

½ cup chopped fresh parsley

⅓ cup chopped fresh cilantro

Whisk together all dressing ingredients in a small bowl or measuring cup. (Alternatively, you can shake them up in a mason jar or whirl them in a small blender.) Set aside.

Combine all salad ingredients in a large bowl and mix well. Pour dressing over salad and mix gently until all ingredients are well coated. It might seem like a lot of dressing, but the cranberries will soak up some of it. Add a few more grinds of black pepper and a pinch of salt, if desired. Cover and refrigerate for at least 1 hour before serving (or up to 1 day). This salad benefits from some marinating time in the fridge.

Makes about 7 cups salad

Per cup: 279 calories, 12.6 g total fat (1.3 g saturated fat), 10.7 g protein, 34.5 g carbohydrate (6.7 g fiber, 11.6 g sugars), 0 mg cholesterol, 235 mg sodium

Despite being over 90 percent water, cucumbers are important to this salad, so I never leave them out. However, some cucumbers are really seedy characters, and seeds are a no-no. That's why I suggest English cucumbers, which contain fewer seeds. However, if they're available, use those little cukes they sell in a pack of five or six. I slice them lengthwise into four pieces, then chop, chop, chop with my chef's knife until they're smaller than diced but bigger than minced.

SWAP IT
Use fresh dill instead of cilantro, but reduce the quantity to 3 tbsp.
TOP IT
Sprinkle crumbled feta cheese on individual servings.

THE Bean Queen's GUIDE to Cooking from Dried

1. INSPECT.

Check for stowaways. Sometimes pebbles and dirt sneak in. Pick out any obvious duds.

2. SOAK.

Place beans in a bowl, cover with 2 inches of cold water and soak overnight. Dried beans are tough little guys—soaking helps to soften them so they cook faster. (Lentils don't need to be soaked.)

3. ADD SPICE, GIRL.

Drain and rinse the beans. Transfer beans to a pot and cover with 2 inches of water. Add aromatics: garlic, onions, bay leaves, rosemary, thyme, black peppercorns or whatever makes your taste buds sing. No one said beans can't be posh. Note: It's better to salt beans *after* they're tender.

Canned beans are *can*venient, but when it comes to taste and texture, dried beans can't be beat.

4. SIMMER DOWN.

Bring to a boil, reduce heat, cover and *gently* simmer the beans until tender, anywhere from 20 minutes (lentils) to 2 hours, depending on the type of bean. Skim off foam.

5. COOL BEANS.

Drain the beans, discard the aromatics and let them cool. Ta-da! You're ready to turn humble cooked beans into something magical! Refrigerate beans for up to 5 days or freeze cooked beans in little baggies.

Beans

Tuscan Tuna & White Bean Salad

with tomatoes, cucumbers and fresh herbs

GF DF

If you're looking for an "I'm-starving-and-don't-feel-like-fussing" lunchtime salad recipe, this is it! Healthy, simple, delicious, filling (lots of fiber and protein), makes great leftovers—I'd eat this salad every day if given the oppor-tuna-ty.

Salad

2 cans (19 oz/540 mL each) no-salt-added white kidney (cannellini) beans, drained and rinsed

2 cans (6 oz/170 g each) water-packed tuna, drained (see Kitchen Whizdom)

1½ cups halved cherry or grape tomatoes

1½ cups peeled, diced English cucumbers

½ cup minced or thinly sliced red onions

3 tbsp minced fresh dill or chopped fresh basil (or a bit of both!)

Dressing

¼ cup olive oil

2 tbsp red wine vinegar

2 tbsp freshly squeezed lemon juice

2 tsp liquid honey

1 tsp Dijon mustard

1 tsp minced garlic

¼ tsp sea salt

⅛ tsp freshly ground black pepper

In a large bowl, combine beans, drained tuna, tomatoes, cucumbers, red onions and dill. Stir gently to avoid smashing the beans.

Make the dressing: In a small bowl or measuring cup, whisk together all dressing ingredients until well blended. Pour over salad and mix well. Add more salt and freshly ground black pepper to taste. Serve immediately or chill before serving.

Makes about 8 cups salad

Per cup: 208 calories, 7.2 g total fat (1.1 g saturated fat), 16.4 g protein, 21.8 g carbohydrate (7.7 g fiber, 3.2 g sugars), 15 mg cholesterol, 105 mg sodium

I use solid white albacore tuna for this recipe because it breaks apart in bigger pieces versus tiny flakes. Tiny flakes are fine for a tuna sandwich, but not for a salad, in my humble opinion. Look for solid albacore tuna on sale, since it's a bit more expensive than flaked tuna. If you prefer, you can use tuna packed in olive oil. Just make sure you drain the oil before mixing the tuna with the beans.

PERFECTION *from* PANTRY STAPLES

SWAP IT

Use chickpeas or navy beans instead of cannellini beans.

TOP IT

If you're a feta fanatic like I am, it's a great addition to this salad.

Mediterranean Lentil & Chickpea Salad

with chopped veggies and fresh parsley

GF

Beans

If you're a fan of Greek salad, you'll love this colorful, flavor-packed version that includes high-fiber, protein-boosting lentils and chickpeas. Extra hungry? Serve this salad as a super side dish to grilled fish, chicken or steak. And call me when you make it. I'm coming over!

Salad

1 can (19 oz/540 mL) no-salt-added chickpeas, drained and rinsed

1 can (19 oz/540 mL) lentils, drained and rinsed

1½ cups halved cherry or grape tomatoes

1½ cups diced English cucumbers

1 cup crumbled light or regular feta cheese (4 oz/113 g)

½ cup pitted Kalamata olives (Love olives? Add more!)

½ cup diced or very thinly sliced red onions

⅓ cup chopped fresh parsley

2 tbsp minced fresh dill*

1 medium avocado, diced or sliced (optional)

Dressing

¼ cup olive oil

3 tbsp red wine vinegar

1 tbsp freshly squeezed lemon juice

2 tsp liquid honey

1 tsp minced garlic

1 tsp Dijon mustard

½ tsp dried oregano

¼ tsp each sea salt and freshly ground black pepper

***You can use fresh mint instead of dill, but increase the quantity to ¼ cup.**

Combine all salad ingredients in a large bowl and mix well.

Make the dressing: Whisk together all dressing ingredients in a small bowl or measuring cup. Pour over salad and stir gently. Cover and refrigerate for at least 2 hours before serving.

Makes about 9 cups salad

Per cup: 221 calories, 11 g total fat (2.6 g saturated fat), 10.2 g protein, 20.3 g carbohydrate (5 g fiber, 2.9 g sugars), 6 mg cholesterol, 411 mg sodium

SWAP IT

You can use just chickpeas or just lentils—you don't need to mix them.

TOP IT

To increase the protein content, add some drained, canned tuna.

Navy Bean & Chickpea Salad

with sun-dried tomatoes and red wine vinaigrette

This tasty little number looks like an edible bowl of confetti, though you don't need a special occasion to justify making it. Borrowing some flavor-infused oil from the sun-dried tomatoes adds punch to the vinaigrette. Bonus: You can store this salad in the fridge for days and it won't deteriorate—it'll just stay delicious!

Salad

1 can (19 oz/540 mL) no-salt-added navy beans, drained and rinsed

1 can (19 oz/540 mL) no-salt-added chickpeas, drained and rinsed

⅔ cup each finely chopped red and green bell peppers

⅓ cup minced red onions

⅓ cup chopped fresh parsley

¼ cup finely chopped oil-packed sun-dried tomatoes

Dressing

2 tbsp olive oil

2 tbsp oil from sun-dried tomatoes

3 tbsp red wine vinegar

1 tbsp freshly squeezed lemon juice

2 tsp Dijon mustard

2 tsp pure maple syrup

1 tsp minced garlic

½ tsp dried basil

¼ tsp each sea salt and freshly ground black pepper

Combine all salad ingredients in a large bowl. Set aside.

Whisk together all dressing ingredients in a small bowl or measuring cup. Pour over salad and mix well. Add a few more grinds of black pepper and mix again. Serve immediately or cover and refrigerate (up to 1 day) before serving.

Makes about 6 cups salad

Per cup: 286 calories, 12 g total fat (1.6 g saturated fat), 10.3 g protein, 36.9 g carbohydrate (11.5 g fiber, 3.2 g sugars), 0 mg cholesterol, 172 mg sodium

SWITCH IT UP

Try this recipe with my pesto vinaigrette on page 120.

JAZZ IT UP

Add 1 tbsp minced fresh dill to the salad.

Pinto Bean, Tomato & Avocado Salad

with white balsamic-lime vinaigrette

Don't you just love a low-effort, high-reward recipe? This easy, breezy bean salad with Tex-Mex flair from the pintos, avocado and cilantro can be whipped together quickly and tastes surprisingly delicious for something so simple (thanks to the oh-so-tasty dressing!).

Dressing

¼ cup avocado oil or olive oil

3 tbsp white balsamic vinegar

1 tbsp freshly squeezed lime juice

1 tbsp pure maple syrup

1 tsp minced garlic

½ tsp Dijon mustard

½ tsp grated lime zest

½ tsp sea salt

¼ tsp each ground cumin, smoked paprika and freshly ground black pepper

Salad

2 cans (19 oz/540 mL each) no-salt-added pinto beans, drained and rinsed (see Kitchen Whizdom)

2 cups halved or quartered cherry tomatoes

½ cup thinly sliced or diced red onions

⅓ cup chopped fresh cilantro

1 large avocado, diced

Whisk together all dressing ingredients in a small bowl or measuring cup. Set aside.

Combine all salad ingredients in a large bowl and mix very gently to avoid squishing the beans. Add dressing and mix again. Salad may be served immediately or refrigerated until ready to serve. If making ahead, dice and add the avocado just before serving.

Makes about 7 cups salad

Per cup: 278 calories, 12.7 g total fat (1.6 g saturated fat), 10.6 g protein, 32.7 g carbohydrate (10.6 g fiber, 5.4 g sugars), 0 mg cholesterol, 200 mg sodium

Where have pinto beans been all my life? They're rich and creamy and kinda buttery, known mostly for their starring role in Mexican refried beans. With 15 g fiber and 15 g protein per cup, they're an excellent source of plant-based nutrition. Just a heads-up, pintos are softer (more delicate) than most other beans, so you need to be gentle with them while mixing. Banged-up beans aren't the best looking, but they're still tasty.

SWITCH IT UP
Don't like cilantro?
Use fresh parsley.
JAZZ IT UP
Add 1 cup diced
cucumbers for a bit
of crunch.

Simple Summery Chickpea Salad

with diced avocados and fresh dill

DF

Drumroll, please! Let me present the tastiest, easiest summer salad recipe ever! If you have cherry tomatoes and cucumbers growing in your garden, now's your chance to use them. This super-healthy salad is one of my most-shared recipes on social media.

Dressing

2 tbsp olive oil

2 tbsp freshly squeezed lemon juice

1 tbsp balsamic vinegar

1 tbsp minced fresh dill

1 tsp Dijon mustard

1 tsp pure maple syrup

Salad

1 can (19 oz/540 mL) no-salt-added chickpeas, drained and rinsed

1½ cups peeled, diced English cucumbers

1½ cups halved cherry tomatoes

¼ cup minced or very thinly sliced red onions (see Kitchen Whizdom)

1 medium avocado, diced

Sea salt and freshly ground black pepper to taste

Whisk together all dressing ingredients in a small bowl or measuring cup. Set aside.

Combine all salad ingredients in a large bowl, being careful not to squish the avocado. Add the dressing and mix well. Add a couple pinches of sea salt and a few grinds of freshly ground black pepper. Mix again and serve immediately.

Makes about 6 cups salad

Per cup: 184 calories, 9.5 g total fat (1.3 g saturated fat), 5.5 g protein, 21 g carbohydrate (5.2 g fiber, 4 g sugars), 0 mg cholesterol, 116 mg sodium

Wanna take the sharp bite out of raw onions? It's easy. Just slice them thinly, then soak the onions in a bowl of very cold water for about 20 minutes. Soaking helps reduce the sulfur compounds that make raw onions so potent. This creates a mellower flavor that's less pungent and more palatable for some people.

make it in Minutes
SWAP IT
Try lime juice and cilantro instead of lemon juice and dill.
TOP IT
Some crumbled feta cheese would taste great!

Beans

Feta Bruschetta Lentil Salad

with fresh basil and balsamic vinaigrette

GF

Garden overflowing with basil and tomatoes? Have I got a salad for you! My warm feta bruschetta from "Yum & Yummer" was wildly popular, likely because it's easy to make yet loaded with flavor. This cold variation combines that delicious bruschetta with finely diced cucumbers and high-protein, high-fiber lentils for a quick lunch salad or a scrumptious side dish.

Dressing

3 tbsp olive oil

3 tbsp balsamic vinegar

1 tbsp freshly squeezed lemon juice

1 tbsp pure maple syrup

1 tsp Dijon mustard

¼ tsp sea salt

⅛ tsp freshly ground black pepper

Salad

2 cans (19 oz/540 mL each) lentils, drained and rinsed

2 cups diced tomatoes (see Kitchen Whizdom)

1 cup diced English cucumbers (small dice)

¾ cup diced red onions

2 tsp minced garlic

1 cup crumbled light or regular feta cheese (4 oz/113 g)

12 large basil leaves, chopped

Whisk together all dressing ingredients in a small bowl or measuring cup. (Alternatively, you can shake them up in a mason jar or whirl them in a small blender.) Set aside.

Combine all salad ingredients in a large bowl and mix well. Pour dressing over salad and mix gently until all ingredients are well coated. Add a few more grinds of black pepper and serve immediately. If preparing this salad in advance, chop and add the fresh basil just before serving.

Makes about 8 cups salad

Per cup: 195 calories, 7.3 g total fat (2.2 g saturated fat), 12 g protein, 21.8 g carbohydrate (5.3 g fiber, 4.3 g sugars), 7 mg cholesterol, 374 mg sodium

Bruschetta tastes best when it's made with any variety of ripe summer tomatoes. However, if you're craving bruschetta outside of tomato season, buy cherry tomatoes, since they're consistently sweet all year round. Note: Don't refrigerate tomatoes! You probably already know this, but I'll say it anyway: Refrigerating tomatoes zaps them of their flavor. I keep tomatoes in a bowl on my kitchen counter and use them within a couple days.

SWITCH IT UP

Use canned chickpeas instead of lentils.

JAZZ IT UP

Try oregano-flavored feta cheese instead of plain feta.

Beans

Warm White Bean & Bacon Salad

with smoky red wine vinaigrette

GF DF

Perfect for chilly weather, this warm, comforting bean salad with a hint of smoked paprika is a delicious accompaniment to roasted meats, chicken or sausages.

- **4 slices thick-cut bacon (about 8 oz/227 g; see Kitchen Whizdom)**
- **1 cup diced red onions**
- **2 tsp minced garlic**
- **3 tbsp red wine vinegar**
- **1 tbsp Dijon mustard**
- **1 tbsp pure maple syrup**
- **½ tsp smoked paprika**
- **¼ tsp freshly ground black pepper**
- **2 cans (19 oz/540 mL each) no-salt-added white kidney (cannellini) beans, drained and rinsed**
- **1 cup halved or quartered cherry tomatoes**
- **¼ cup chopped fresh cilantro or parsley**

Note: You'll need a deep, 10-inch nonstick skillet for this recipe.

Chop bacon into smallish, bite-sized pieces and separate pieces so they aren't stuck together. Heat a deep, 10-inch nonstick skillet over medium heat and add bacon. Cook until bacon is crispy but not crunchy (done to your liking) and fat has been rendered. Don't rush it and do not discard the fat! You'll need it for the dressing.

Add onions and garlic to bacon in skillet. Cook and stir for 2 more minutes, just to take the raw edge off the onions. Add vinegar, mustard, maple syrup, paprika and pepper. Mix well and cook for 1 more minute. Add beans and mix gently until beans are coated with dressing.

Remove skillet from heat and stir in tomatoes and cilantro. Add a few more grinds of black pepper and serve immediately. Once left to sit or refrigerated, the dressing will solidify, so this salad must be served warm.

Makes 8 side-dish servings

Per serving: 214 calories, 9.2 g total fat (4 g saturated fat), 12.3 g protein, 21.7 g carbohydrate (7.4 g fiber, 3 g sugars), 17 mg cholesterol, 187 mg sodium

Please don't use turkey bacon or lean bacon for this recipe. It won't work, since the dressing depends on the rendered fat and flavor from the bacon drippings. You're splurging here, remember? This isn't a recipe I'd make often but, every once in a while, there's room for an "Ah, what the heck!" indulgence.

Wickedly Delicious
Splurge-Worthy
Totally Worth It!
A quick & easy comfort-food salad

Beans

White Bean Tabbouleh-ish Salad

with fresh herbs and white balsamic vinaigrette

Adding cute little navy beans (packed with plant-based protein and fiber) to Lebanese tabbouleh turns a light side salad into a satisfying lunch. Tabbouleh is basically a celebration of herbs (parsley and mint) and I'm inviting you to join the party! Purists will say that radishes and vinegar don't belong in tabbouleh, but neither do white beans, sooo....

Dressing

3 tbsp olive oil

2 tbsp white balsamic vinegar

2 tbsp freshly squeezed lemon juice

2 tsp pure maple syrup

1 tsp minced garlic

1 tsp grated lemon zest

½ tsp Dijon mustard

¼ tsp each sea salt and freshly ground black pepper

Salad

1 can (19 oz/540 mL) no-salt-added navy beans, drained and rinsed

2 cups seeded, diced Roma (plum) tomatoes (see Kitchen Whizdom)

2 cups seeded, diced cucumbers (peeled or unpeeled)

1 cup chopped fresh curly parsley

½ cup chopped fresh mint

½ cup minced red onions

½ cup minced radishes

Whisk together all dressing ingredients in a small bowl or measuring cup. Set aside.

Combine all salad ingredients in a large bowl and mix well. Pour dressing over salad and mix gently until all ingredients are well coated. Serve immediately or cover and chill for 1 to 2 hours before serving.

Makes about 7 cups salad

Per cup: 162 calories, 6.5 g total fat (0.8 g saturated fat), 5.3 g protein, 22 g carbohydrate (7.5 g fiber, 4.3 g sugars), 0 mg cholesterol, 115 mg sodium

Halve the plum tomatoes lengthwise and squeeze out the juice and seeds before dicing into small pieces. For most salads, this step is unnecessary, but for tabbouleh, you don't want the extra liquid to make the salad soggy or watery. Quartered grape tomatoes are a good substitute for plum tomatoes in this recipe.

SWITCH IT UP
Use chopped green onions instead of red onions.
tabbouleh GETS A bean boost
JAZZ IT UP
Add one small diced yellow, orange or red bell pepper.

CHAPTER 5

THE CLASSICS

If it ain't broke, don't fix it!

(Let's be honest, I'm probably going to fix it. Old-school gets a new vibe in some of these timeless treasures.)

My Big Fat Greek Salad

with a simple red wine vinaigrette

GF

Am I allowed to say a recipe is stupidly easy to make? Because a traditional, no-lettuce-allowed Greek salad is so simple yet somehow ends up tasting like food for the gods. No wonder it's a classic and one of my absolute favorites! In Greece, they drizzle the salad with their rich, luscious olive oil and a splash of red wine vinegar. That's it. But I've created a dressing that tastes similar to Greek dressings served at restaurants.

Salad

3 cups chopped tomatoes (see Kitchen Whizdom)

2 cups diced English cucumbers (peeled or unpeeled)

1 large green bell pepper, sliced or chopped

4 oz (113 g) light or regular feta cheese, cubed or coarsely crumbled

½ cup very thinly sliced red onions

½ cup pitted Kalamata olives

Dressing

¼ cup olive oil

3 tbsp red wine vinegar

1 tsp minced garlic

1 tsp Dijon mustard

1 tsp granulated sugar

1 tsp dried oregano, plus extra for sprinkling

½ tsp sea salt

¼ tsp freshly ground black pepper

Combine all salad ingredients in a large bowl. Be careful not to squish the feta. For traditional Greek salad, the cheese is better in cubes or chunks than crumbles. Set aside.

Whisk together all dressing ingredients in a small bowl or measuring cup. Pour over salad and mix well. Sprinkle a bit more dried oregano and freshly ground black pepper over the salad and serve immediately.

Makes about 7 cups salad

Per cup: 170 calories, 13.2 g total fat (3.2 g saturated fat), 5.4 g protein, 6.9 g carbohydrate (2 g fiber, 4.3 g sugars), 8 mg cholesterol, 575 mg sodium

In the off-season when tomatoes aren't at their peak, I recommend using cherry tomatoes or Campari tomatoes, which taste great all year long. However, the BEST Greek salads use the freshest possible vine-ripened tomatoes. I believe the quality and freshness of the vegetables are what make this salad shine.

SWAP IT
Sprinkle 2 tsp minced fresh oregano over the salad instead of dried oregano.
When life gives you olives...
TOP IT
Please forgive me, my Greek friends, but sometimes I add diced avocados just before serving.

Classics

Caesar Pleaser Salad

with rich, creamy dressing and sourdough croutons

Almost everyone loves a good Caesar, making it one of the most popular salads in the world, with endless variations and interpretations. Authentic Caesar dressing starts with olive oil thickened with raw eggs to create mayonnaise, but we'll use an olive oil and mayo combo, which is easier and basically foolproof. Some would call this a lazy Caesar, but I think it's an amaze-y Caesar!

Dressing

¾ cup light mayonnaise

⅓ cup freshly grated Parmesan cheese (see Kitchen Whizdom)

2 tbsp olive oil

2 tbsp freshly squeezed lemon juice

2 tsp minced garlic (Love garlic? Add more!)

1 tsp anchovy paste

1 tsp Worcestershire sauce

1 tsp Dijon mustard

¼ tsp freshly ground black pepper

Salad

1 large head or 2 small heads romaine lettuce, torn or chopped

8 slices bacon, cooked and chopped*

2 cups Sourdough Croutons (see recipe, page 249)

Shaved or freshly grated Parmesan for serving

Add all dressing ingredients to the bowl of a mini food processor and whirl until smooth. Alternatively, if you do a really good job of whisking the ingredients together in a small bowl like your life depends on it, I'll forgive you. ☺ Cover and refrigerate the dressing overnight. It tastes so much better after chilling for a minimum of 12 hours.

Place all salad ingredients except Parmesan in a large bowl and toss to combine. Add the dressing and mix well using tongs. Top individual servings with shaved Parmesan and a few extra grinds of black pepper. This is an important final touch.

Makes 6 servings

Per serving: 299 calories, 21 g total fat (4.8 g saturated fat), 10.5 g protein, 16.5 g carbohydrate (2 g fiber, 1.1 g sugars), 24 mg cholesterol, 610 mg sodium*

*To reduce the sodium content, use reduced-sodium bacon.

When it comes to choosing Parmesan cheese for Caesar salad, it's best to use the "good stuff," which is imported Parmigiano-Reggiano from Italy. According to the Parmigiano Reggiano Consortium (an actual thing!), this richly flavored cheese is in a class by itself, and once you compare it to regular Parmesan, you'll understand. Look for the Parmigiano-Reggiano name emblazoned on the rind—you can't miss it! If you're buying a container of pre-grated Parmesan, the premium stuff will be labeled "Parmigiano-Reggiano," not "Parmesan."

SWITCH IT UP

Try Little Gem lettuce (mini romaine—so cute!) instead of regular romaine lettuce.

JAZZ IT UP

For a main-course Caesar, top this salad with slices of grilled or baked chicken breasts.

Classics

The Beloved Caprese Salad

with homemade balsamic glaze

GF

You hardly need a recipe for this classic Italian masterpiece, but I had to include it because it's one of my all-time favorites. How can something so simple be so delicious? Freshness! Peak-season tomatoes, fresh basil and a big ball of fresh mozzarella. Magnifico!

⅓ cup balsamic vinegar

1 tbsp brown sugar

4 medium freshly picked or on-the-vine tomatoes, sliced

12 oz (340 g) fresh mozzarella cheese, sliced*

1 tbsp olive oil

Sea salt and freshly ground black pepper to taste

Fresh basil leaves

***Use a very sharp knife to slice the soft mozzarella so it doesn't get squished. Slice the tomatoes and mozzarella to the same thickness. See photo for reference.**

Make the balsamic glaze: Whisk together balsamic vinegar and brown sugar in your smallest pot or skillet over medium-high heat. When mixture comes to a boil, reduce heat immediately to a gentle simmer. Turn on your vent hood—simmering vinegar can smell quite strong! Let the mixture simmer (not boil) until it begins to get syrupy and reduces in quantity by about half, whisking occasionally. This should take no more than 5 minutes. It will coat the pan or skillet if you swirl it around. Remove from heat and cool slightly before serving. It'll thicken a bit as it cools, so keep this in mind. If you accidentally thicken it too much, you can thin it with water.

To assemble salad, alternate layers of sliced tomatoes and mozzarella on a serving dish, as shown in photo. Drizzle with olive oil, sprinkle with salt and pepper, then drizzle with 2 tbsp balsamic glaze. Top with fresh basil (either whole leaves or chiffonade cut). Serve immediately with extra glaze on the side.

Makes 8 side-dish servings

Per serving: 155 calories, 10.3 g total fat (5.2 g saturated fat), 9 g protein, 6 g carbohydrate (0.5 g fiber, 4.9 g sugars), 28 mg cholesterol, 75 mg sodium

Truth be told, an authentic Caprese salad doesn't contain balsamic vinegar at all, let alone a balsamic glaze. But it's a formula for deliciousness when this sticky-sweet, bold sauce is drizzled over tomatoes and fresh mozzarella. You can double or triple the glaze recipe and store it in an airtight container in the fridge, but you'll need to simmer it a bit longer for the vinegar to thicken. If purchasing premade balsamic glaze, I highly suggest Nonna Pia's brand.

SWITCH IT UP

Multicolored heirloom tomatoes make for an even prettier presentation. Tomatoes not in season? Try my roasted beet version on page 206.

JAZZ IT UP

Add sliced avocados between the cheese and tomatoes.

The Iconic Cobb Salad

with chicken, bacon, eggs and avocados

GF

The famous Cobb salad is often served with a simple red wine vinaigrette, since heavy salads usually benefit from lighter dressings. I've added minced shallots and a hint of creaminess from light mayonnaise in my version. Ranch dressing lovers might prefer its stronger flavor on a Cobb salad and balsamic die-hards won't be disappointed if they stick with their favorite, too. I say choose the dressing you love and go for it!

Dressing

⅓ cup olive oil

¼ cup red wine vinegar

2 tbsp light mayonnaise

1 tbsp freshly squeezed lemon juice

1 tbsp pure maple syrup or liquid honey

1 tbsp minced shallots

2 tsp Dijon mustard

1 tsp minced garlic

½ tsp each dried Italian seasoning and sea salt

¼ tsp freshly ground black pepper

Salad

8 cups chopped romaine or mixed lettuces

3 cups chopped cooked chicken breast

8 slices bacon, cooked and chopped

1½ cups halved cherry tomatoes

3 hard-boiled eggs, quartered

2 medium avocados, sliced or diced

1 cup crumbled blue cheese (4 oz/113 g)*

***For a strong blue-cheese flavor, go with Roquefort (France). For milder flavor, use Gorgonzola (Italian).**

Whisk together all dressing ingredients in a small bowl or shake them up in a mason jar. If you own a single-serve blender, now would be the time to use it, since it makes the dressing so silky and smooth. Refrigerate dressing until ready to use.

Combine all salad ingredients except blue cheese in a very large bowl, slicing and adding the avocados last since they brown quickly. Add the dressing and mix well. Top individual servings with crumbled blue cheese. Serve immediately.

Makes 6 servings

Per serving: Never mind. (No, really, just forget about it.)

SWAP IT

Not a fan of blue cheese? Use feta instead. Try sliced, grilled steak or pan-seared salmon instead of chicken.

TOP IT

Sprinkle with minced fresh chives, the traditional garnish for Cobb salad.

Everyone's Favorite Creamy Coleslaw

with a mayo-based, tangy-sweet dressing

GF

My mother, Alfreda, was the best cook and instinctively knew how to make just about anything without a recipe. Her creamy coleslaw appeared at every backyard BBQ party and was gobbled up in minutes. Lucky for me, this is one recipe she actually wrote down. The only changes I've made are adding some finely diced red bell peppers and switching the plain, white vinegar to apple cider vinegar. And, for convenience, I use bagged coleslaw mix.

Dressing

½ cup mayonnaise (light or regular)

¼ cup 14% (full-fat) sour cream

2 tbsp granulated sugar

1 tbsp apple cider vinegar

1 tbsp freshly squeezed lemon juice

1 tsp dry mustard or 2 tsp Dijon mustard

½ tsp celery seed

½ tsp sea salt

⅛ tsp freshly ground black pepper

Salad

1 bag (1 lb/454 g) coleslaw mix (see Kitchen Whizdom)

½ cup finely diced celery

½ cup finely diced red bell peppers

½ cup chopped green onions

Whisk together all dressing ingredients in a small bowl or measuring cup. Cover and refrigerate until ready to use.

In a large bowl, combine coleslaw mix, celery, bell peppers and green onions. Add dressing and mix well. Cover and refrigerate for at least 4 hours for the best flavor. Mix well before serving. Coleslaw dressing tends to sink to the bottom of the salad over time so give it a good stir before serving.

Makes about 5 cups salad

Per ½ cup: 70 calories, 4.2 g total fat (0.7 g saturated fat), 1.9 g protein, 7.6 g carbohydrate (1.8 g fiber, 3.2 g sugars), 2 mg cholesterol, 255 mg sodium

Bagged coleslaw mix is a combination of shredded green cabbage, red cabbage and carrots. It's convenient and relatively inexpensive, when you consider the cost of buying an entire green cabbage and a whole red cabbage, only to use a part of each for this recipe. Empty the contents of the bagged slaw onto a large cutting board, spread it out and chop it up with a chef's knife so the pieces are smaller and more uniform. No big chunks of cabbage allowed! If you prefer all ingredients from scratch (great!), you'll need about 4 to 5 cups of finely shredded green cabbage and roughly ¾ cup each finely shredded red cabbage and grated carrots.

SWITCH IT UP
Use broccoli slaw mix
instead of coleslaw mix.
JAZZ IT UP
Slice 5 small Brussels
sprouts paper thin and add
them to the mix.

Italian Chopped Salad

with a bright and bold red wine vinaigrette

GF

It's an everything-but-the-kitchen-sink salad, Italian style! Grab your cutting board, a good sharp knife, put on some tunes and let's get chopping!

Dressing

⅓ cup olive oil

¼ cup red wine vinegar

2 tbsp light mayonnaise

1 tbsp freshly squeezed lemon juice

1 tbsp pure maple syrup or liquid honey

1 tbsp minced shallots

2 tsp Dijon mustard

1 tsp minced garlic

1 tsp dried oregano

½ tsp sea salt

¼ tsp freshly ground black pepper

Salad

6 cups chopped iceberg or romaine lettuce

4 oz (113 g) diced salami

4 oz (113 g) diced Provolone or aged white cheddar cheese

1½ cups quartered grape or cherry tomatoes

1½ cups diced English cucumbers

1 cup diced yellow bell peppers

1 cup no-salt-added canned chickpeas, drained and rinsed

½ cup pitted Kalamata olives

½ cup chopped radicchio

⅓ cup thinly sliced red onions

⅓ cup freshly grated or shaved Parmesan cheese

Whisk together all dressing ingredients in a small bowl or shake them up in a mason jar. If you own a single-serve blender, whirl the ingredients to make the dressing extra silky. Refrigerate dressing until ready to use.

Combine all salad ingredients except Parmesan in a very large serving bowl. Add dressing and mix well. Add the Parmesan just before serving, either mixed into the salad or sprinkled over individual servings.

Makes about 12 cups salad

Per cup: 161 calories, 11.5 g total fat (2.5 g saturated fat), 6.3 g protein, 8.4 g carbohydrate (2.2 g fiber, 3.2 g sugars), 10 mg cholesterol, 355 mg sodium

SWAP IT

I personally LOVE aged white cheddar in this recipe, but mini bocconcini would also work well.

TOP IT

If you're a fan of nippy pepperoncini peppers, chop two or three and sprinkle them over the salad before serving.

Classics

Tabbouleh with a Twist

A salad for herb lovers

GF * DF V *

Fluffy, light and refreshing, Middle Eastern tabbouleh is a super-green, herby salad loaded with fresh parsley and mint, with a small amount of grain thrown into the mix. My "Greta-cized" recipe might not be considered authentic, but it's still super scrumptious, blending elements of traditional Lebanese tabbouleh with hints of its Moroccan counterpart. A luscious, lemony dressing makes this super-healthy salad herbaceously delicious!

Salad

4 cups chopped fresh curly parsley (1 extra-large bunch or 2 medium bunches)

1½ cups cooked whole wheat couscous, quinoa or bulgur wheat

1 cup diced English cucumbers

1 cup quartered grape tomatoes or diced Roma (plum) tomatoes

½ cup chopped green onions

½ cup chopped fresh mint

Dressing

⅓ cup olive oil

3 tbsp freshly squeezed lemon juice

1 tbsp white balsamic vinegar

2 tsp liquid honey or pure maple syrup

1 tsp minced garlic (more if you love garlic!)

¼ tsp sea salt

⅛ tsp freshly ground black pepper

Combine all salad ingredients in a large bowl. Set aside.

Whisk together all dressing ingredients in a small bowl or measuring cup. Pour over salad and mix well using tongs, until all ingredients are coated with dressing.

For best results, cover and refrigerate the salad for 30 minutes before serving.

Makes about 7 cups salad

Per cup: 188 calories, 11 g total fat (1.5 g saturated fat), 3.5 g protein, 19 g carbohydrate (2.8 g fiber, 3.7 g sugars), 0 mg cholesterol, 104 mg sodium

***For gluten-free, use quinoa instead of couscous or bulgur. For vegan, use pure maple syrup instead of honey.**

Tabbouleh is basically a parsley salad, making this herb the star of the recipe. Buy the freshest, most beautiful "bouquet" of parsley you can find, rinse it well with cold water and dry it thoroughly (with paper towels or a salad spinner) before chopping it up. I prefer curly parsley to flat-leaf parsley for this recipe, since the curly variety maintains its fluffiness, even after it's coated with dressing. If using Roma tomatoes, squeeze out the juice and seeds before dicing, otherwise the salad could get a bit soggy.

SWAP IT

Use white wine vinegar instead of white balsamic vinegar.

Herbalicious flavor!

TOP IT

Sprinkle with toasted pine nuts and pomegranate seeds before serving for an elevated, holiday-inspired twist.

Classics

The One with the Ramen Noodles

and the lip-smacking, sweet sesame dressing

DF V

Not sure what to feed your F•R•I•E•N•D•S at your next social gathering? Make sure the menu includes this relatable, reliable, really delicious mix of crunchy veggies, toasted almonds and crushed ramen noodles with an addictively sweet, sesame-ginger dressing. Popular for decades, yet not exactly gourmet fare, people always go nuts for this retro recipe.

Salad

2 pkgs (3 oz/85 g each) ramen noodles, broken up (see Kitchen Whizdom)

1 cup sliced almonds

7 cups very thinly sliced Savoy cabbage

2 cups very thinly sliced red cabbage

2 cans (10 oz/284 mL each) mandarin orange segments in light syrup, drained, or 1½ cups diced fresh mango

1½ cups grated carrots

1 cup chopped green onions

⅓ cup chopped fresh cilantro

Dressing

½ cup neutral-tasting oil, such as sunflower or safflower oil (I use organic)

¼ cup seasoned rice vinegar

¼ cup Thai sweet chili sauce

1½ tbsp dark sesame oil

1 tbsp freshly squeezed lime juice

1 tbsp reduced-sodium soy sauce

1 tbsp grated fresh gingerroot

2 tsp minced garlic

Place the broken ramen noodles and almonds in a dry, 10-inch nonstick skillet over medium-low heat. Cook and stir until the noodles and almonds are lightly toasted. Be careful not to burn them. Remove from heat and transfer to a large mixing bowl to cool.

While the noodles and almonds are cooling, make the dressing: Whisk together all dressing ingredients in a small bowl or measuring cup, or shake them up in a mason jar. Set aside.

Add all remaining salad ingredients to the bowl with noodles and almonds. Add the dressing and mix again using tongs, until all ingredients are well coated with dressing. May be served immediately or covered and refrigerated until ready to serve. I prefer this salad chilled before serving.

Makes about 14 cups salad

Per cup: 178 calories, 12.6 g total fat (1.4 g saturated fat), 3.3 g protein, 13.9 g carbohydrate (2.5 g fiber, 5.9 g sugars), 0 mg cholesterol, 113 mg sodium

For the ramen, you'll need two packages of the 99-cent noodles you survived on as a broke student. Throw out the seasoning pack. To crush the ramen, leave it in the package, place it on a cutting board and gently pound it (oxymoron?) with a rolling pin or meat mallet. You don't want crumbs, just broken up pieces.

SWITCH IT UP

Use roasted, salted sunflower seeds instead of almonds. (No need to toast them.)

JAZZ IT UP

Mix in some chopped rotisserie chicken for an easy dinner.

Why HEIRLOOMS are the Jacqueline Kennedy Onassis OF TOMATOES

1. Unique and Varied Beauty.

Jackie was known for her individuality and striking beauty, much like heirloom tomatoes, which come in diverse shapes, sizes and colors, each with its own charm.

2. Timeless Appeal.

Just as Jackie O's classic style transcended eras (Hello, pillbox hat!), heirloom tomatoes are prized for their lasting allure and a history worth savoring (and saving).

3. Effortless Class.

Jackie had a knack for making simplicity look luxurious, just as a simple heirloom tomato can elevate a salad with its striking appearance and rich flavor.

4. One of a Kind.

Heirloom tomatoes, like Jackie O, stand apart from the ordinary and are in a league of their own.

5. Iconic Status.

Both Jackie O and heirloom tomatoes are cultural icons—one in style and sophistication, the other in the culinary world.

Heirloom Tomato Salad, page 208.

Panzanella à la Greta

with oregano, basil and a light vinaigrette

This Tuscan-inspired bread and tomato salad with fresh herbs is the perfect warm-weather dinner pairing for any grilled meats. It's delicious during colder months, too (with a hot bowl of soup), but I love it best with garden-fresh tomatoes at their peak ripeness. To enhance the traditional recipe, I've added some cucumbers for crunch and fresh mozzarella for creamy richness.

Salad

6 cups cubed rustic Italian bread, such as ciabatta (see Kitchen Whizdom)

2 tbsp olive oil

1 lb (454 g) assorted tomatoes, cut into wedges or chunks (or halved cherry tomatoes)

1 medium English cucumber, halved lengthwise and sliced

6 oz (170 g) fresh mozzarella cheese, sliced

½ medium red onion, very thinly sliced

½ cup torn fresh basil leaves

1 tbsp minced fresh oregano

Dressing

¼ cup olive oil

2 tbsp white balsamic vinegar

1 tsp minced garlic

½ tsp Dijon mustard

½ tsp sea salt

¼ tsp freshly ground black pepper

Preheat oven to 350ºF. Line a small, rimmed baking sheet with parchment paper. Arrange bread cubes in a single layer on baking sheet. Drizzle with olive oil and, using your hands, toss cubes until they're evenly coated with oil. Bake for 15 minutes, until bread is lightly toasted and golden. Remove from oven and let cool.

While bread is toasting, whisk together all dressing ingredients in a small bowl or measuring cup. Set aside.

Add toasted bread cubes and all remaining salad ingredients to a large mixing bowl. Drizzle dressing over salad and toss until all ingredients are well coated. Let the salad sit at room temperature for 30 minutes so the bread can absorb the dressing. Mix once or twice during this time. Season with freshly ground black pepper before serving.

Makes 6 side-dish servings

Per serving: 256 calories, 11 g total fat (4.1 g saturated fat), 10.3 g protein, 30 g carbohydrate (2.1 g fiber, 4.1 g sugars), 19 mg cholesterol, 466 mg sodium

You'll need a small loaf of crusty, dense and chewy bread for this recipe. I often buy a ciabatta baguette and use about ¾ of it. Sourdough bread is also delicious. Cut the bread into 1½-inch cubes—like you're making giant croutons. To be specific, last time I made this salad I counted exactly 26 big cubes of bread. ☺ Drying fresh bread in the oven versus using days-old bread means you can make this salad anytime, even with bread that's straight from the bakery.

SWITCH IT UP
Use white or red wine vinegar instead of white balsamic vinegar.
JAZZ IT UP
Make this salad with rosemary focaccia instead of ciabatta and invite me to dinner!

Classics

Perfect Picnic Potato Salad

with a classic rich-and-creamy dressing

GF

Looking for a timeless potato salad recipe that'll be loved and devoured by all? Your search is over! This recipe checks all the boxes: deliciously creamy dressing, a bit of crunch from celery and chopped pickles, plus little flecks of flavor from celery seed, green onions and dill. If there's such a thing as cold comfort food, this is it! (Note: Potato salad almost always tastes better the second day, when the ingredients have had time to mix and mingle.)

Dressing

¾ cup mayonnaise (light or regular)

⅓ cup 14% (full-fat) sour cream

2 tbsp sweet pickle juice (from the jar!)

1 tbsp yellow mustard

1 tsp celery seed

½ tsp sea salt

¼ tsp freshly ground black pepper

Salad

4 lbs (1.81 kg) medium Yukon Gold potatoes

2 tsp sea salt (for boiling potatoes)

4 hard-boiled eggs, mashed

1 cup diced celery

½ cup finely chopped sweet pickles

½ cup chopped green onions

2 tbsp minced fresh dill

Paprika for garnish (optional)

Whisk together all dressing ingredients in a small bowl. Cover and refrigerate until ready to use.

Cut the unpeeled potatoes into quarters and place them in a large pot. Cover potatoes with cold water and bring to a boil. Add salt and reduce heat to medium-low. Simmer, uncovered, until potatoes are tender, but not too soft, about 20 minutes or so, depending on the size of potatoes. Drain potatoes in a colander and spread them onto a large baking sheet to cool. Once cool, peel off the skin and cut potatoes into ¾-inch pieces. Place cut potatoes in a large mixing bowl.

Add all remaining salad ingredients to potatoes and mix gently. Add the dressing and mix again, until all ingredients are well coated. The more you mix, the more mashed the potatoes will become. You decide! Taste and adjust the salt and pepper, if desired. Cover and refrigerate for at least 4 hours before serving. Sprinkle lightly with paprika before serving, if using.

Makes about 10 cups salad

Per ½ cup: 109 calories, 4.1 g total fat (0.8 g saturated fat), 3.1 g protein, 15.6 g carbohydrate (2.4 g fiber, 1.4 g sugars), 38 mg cholesterol, 204 mg sodium

SWAP IT
For more tang, use dill pickles and their juice instead of sweet pickles.

Always a crowd favorite!

TOP IT
Did somebody say chopped bacon?

Classics

The Best Baby Spinach Salad

with warm, bacony, maple-Dijon dressing

Drizzled with a sweet-and-savory, can't-get-enough-of-it warm bacon dressing, I've been devouring this spinach salad for decades and plan to do so until my nursing home refuses to make it for me.

- **1 can (10 oz/284 mL) mandarin orange segments in light syrup, undrained (see Kitchen Whizdom)**
- **8 oz (227 g) fresh baby spinach, stems trimmed (a BIG bowlful!)**
- **3 cups thinly sliced white mushrooms**
- **6 slices bacon**
- **½ cup minced red onions**
- **1 tsp minced garlic**
- **3 tbsp white balsamic vinegar**
- **2 tbsp Dijon mustard**
- **2 tbsp pure maple syrup**
- **Sea salt and freshly ground black pepper to taste**
- **6 hard-boiled eggs, sliced lengthwise into quarters**

Drain the orange segments and reserve the liquid. You should have about ½ cup syrup; set aside. Add drained orange segments to a large mixing bowl, along with the spinach and mushrooms. Set aside.

Cook bacon in a 10-inch nonstick skillet over medium-high heat until crispy but not overcooked. Remove bacon and drain on a paper towel–lined plate. Do not discard bacon drippings. Crumble or chop the bacon and add it to the spinach mixture.

Add onions and garlic to reserved bacon drippings in skillet. Cook and stir over medium-low heat for 1 minute. Add reserved orange syrup and simmer for about 3 minutes. Whisk in vinegar, mustard and maple syrup until well blended. Simmer for 2 more minutes. Remove dressing from heat and add salt and freshly ground black pepper. You should have about 1 cup dressing.

Pour dressing over salad and mix well using tongs. Mound salad on individual serving plates and top with sliced eggs. Serve immediately.

Makes 6 servings

Per serving: 237 calories, 14.4 g total fat (5.5 g saturated fat), 12.7 g protein, 14 g carbohydrate (2 g fiber, 10 g sugars), 202 mg cholesterol, 465 mg sodium

Mandarin orange segments are sold in small cans and in little plastic tubs. For some reason, the tubs do a better job of keeping the segments whole and not squished or broken so, if you see that variety, buy it. Either way, measure ½ cup syrup to make the dressing.

SWAP IT

Use white wine vinegar instead of white balsamic vinegar.

TOP IT

If you like cheese, a light sprinkling of crumbled feta would be tasty!

Mom's 4-Bean Salad

that now contains only 3 beans ☺

GF DF V

Classics

Growing up, I had a deep-seated aversion to my mom's (or any) bean salad. Now that I'm all grown up, I love it! That said, Mom's recipe used four types of beans, including the very scary lima bean, which had no business being served to children. My modified (and slightly modernized) version of Alfreda's salad is lima-less (phew!) but still delicious.

Salad

1 can (19 oz/540 mL) no-salt-added red kidney beans, drained and rinsed

1 can (19 oz/540 mL) no-salt-added chickpeas, drained and rinsed

1½ cups fresh or frozen green beans, cooked (see Kitchen Whizdom)

1 cup diced celery

¾ cup diced green bell peppers

⅔ cup diced sweet onions

⅓ cup chopped fresh parsley

Dressing

¼ cup light-tasting olive oil

¼ cup apple cider vinegar

2 tbsp granulated sugar*

1 tsp Dijon mustard

½ tsp celery seed

¼ tsp each sea salt and freshly ground black pepper

***The sugar is important. Please don't leave it out.**

Combine all salad ingredients in a large bowl and mix well. Set aside.

Whisk together all dressing ingredients in a small bowl or measuring cup until sugar is dissolved. Pour dressing over salad and mix until all ingredients are coated with dressing.

This salad tastes best when refrigerated for at least 4 hours before serving. Overnight "marinating" is even better!

Makes about 8 cups salad

Per cup: 200 calories, 8.2 g total fat (1.2 g saturated fat), 8 g protein, 26.4 g carbohydrate (6.9 g fiber, 5.5 g sugars), 0 mg cholesterol, 107 mg sodium

Many old-fashioned bean salad recipes call for canned green beans and yellow wax beans. I prefer a fresher, slightly crisper green bean—either fresh beans cut into 1-inch pieces or frozen, precut beans that have been steamed until tender-crisp, similar to cooking pasta until al dente. Let the steamed beans cool before adding them to the salad.

HIGH Fiber, HIGH Flavor

SWITCH IT UP

Use red onions instead of sweet onions.

JAZZ IT UP

Add 2 tbsp minced fresh dill to the salad.

Classics

My Wacky Waldorf Salad

with orange-poppy seed dressing

Sweet-and-savory side-dish salads are a hit at potlucks, lunches and holiday brunches, and this delicious Waldorf spin-off is no exception. Crisp apples, crunchy celery and tasty, toasted walnuts pair perfectly with . . . rotini? Yup—that's the wacky part! I've added plump rotini noodles instead of grapes and subbed Greek yogurt for the traditional mayonnaise-laden dressing.

Dressing

¾ cup plain 0% Greek yogurt

¼ cup mayonnaise (light or regular)

1½ tbsp apple cider vinegar

1 tbsp liquid honey

1 tsp poppy seeds

1 tsp grated orange zest

¼ tsp sea salt

⅛ tsp freshly ground black pepper

Salad

8 oz (227 g) uncooked rotini

2 medium Gala or Red Delicious apples, diced

1 cup diced celery

½ cup chopped walnuts or pecans, lightly toasted*

⅓ cup minced red onions

¼ cup chopped fresh parsley

Sea salt and freshly ground black pepper to taste

***If you love walnuts (or pecans), add more. ☺**

Make the dressing: Whisk together all dressing ingredients in a small bowl. Cover and refrigerate until ready to use.

Cook rotini according to package directions. Drain, rinse with cold water (to stop the cooking action) and drain again. Transfer rotini to a large bowl.

Add remaining salad ingredients to cooked rotini and mix well. Add the dressing and mix again, until all ingredients are well coated. Add a bit more salt and pepper, if desired, and serve immediately.

Makes about 8 cups salad

Per cup: 212 calories, 6.8 g total fat (0.6 g saturated fat), 6.8 g protein, 31 g carbohydrate (4.1 g fiber, 7.9 g sugars), 1 mg cholesterol, 149 mg sodium

Make the dressing a few hours (or a day) ahead of time, since it tastes best after chilling in the fridge. Unfortunately, this isn't a "make-ahead" salad, since the noodles really love to soak up the tasty dressing. Who can blame them? However, you can prep all the salad ingredients in advance and toss them with the dressing just before serving.

SWAP IT
Use ½ cup chopped green onions instead of red onions.
TOP IT
Add some chopped, cooked chicken breast for a protein boost.
There's lots of crunch in this noodley lunch!

Warm German Potato Salad

with crispy bacon and a sweet-and-tangy dressing

GF DF

I'm not German, though Greta is a German name. In 2007, I wore a really cute dirndl to Oktoberfest, plus I drive a German car and once adopted a dog that was part German shepherd. Therefore, I'm pretty sure I've earned the right to call my inauthentic (but scrumptious!) version of warm potato salad "German," ja?

3 lbs (1.36 kg) mini red potatoes, halved

6 slices bacon

1¼ cups diced yellow or sweet onions

½ cup finely diced celery

2 tsp minced garlic

⅓ cup dill pickle juice (from the jar!)

2 tbsp grainy Dijon mustard

2 tbsp white balsamic vinegar

1 tbsp olive oil

1 tbsp granulated sugar

½ tsp celery seed

⅓ cup chopped fresh parsley or 3 tbsp minced fresh dill (or some of each)

Freshly ground black pepper to taste

Place halved potatoes in a large pot of cold water and bring to a boil. Reduce heat and simmer, uncovered, until potatoes are fork-tender, about 10 to 12 minutes. Be careful not to overcook them. Drain potatoes, place them in a large mixing bowl and let them cool a bit.

While potatoes are cooling, cook bacon over medium-high heat in a nonstick skillet until done to your liking. (I prefer bacon a bit crispy but not too crunchy.) Remove bacon from skillet, shake excess grease into skillet, and set bacon aside on a paper towel–lined plate. Do not discard the bacon drippings! Reduce heat to medium and add onions and celery to same skillet with bacon drippings. Cook and stir until softened, about 3 minutes. Add garlic and cook for 1 more minute. Add pickle juice, mustard, vinegar, olive oil, sugar and celery seed. Mix well. Bring dressing to a boil, reduce heat and let simmer, uncovered, for 1 minute. Pour hot dressing over potatoes.

Chop the cooked bacon into bite-sized pieces and add to potato mixture, along with parsley. Season with freshly ground black pepper and mix well. Let the salad sit at room temperature for about 20 minutes before serving so the potatoes have time to soak up some dressing.

Makes about 10 cups salad

Per cup: 173 calories, 6.9 g total fat (2.6 g saturated fat), 5 g protein, 23 g carbohydrate (2.8 g fiber, 7 g sugars), 10 mg cholesterol, 198 mg sodium

SWAP IT

Use apple cider vinegar instead of white balsamic for a tangier, more traditional dressing.

TOP IT

Sprinkle with ¼ cup chopped green onions before serving.

Well-Dressed Wedge Salad

with bacon, tomatoes and creamy blue cheese dressing

GF

A permanent fixture on steakhouse menus across the continent, this timeless salad with its BLT vibe and stunning presentation makes an impressive appetizer or spectacular side salad when company's coming.

Dressing

1 cup crumbled blue cheese (4 oz/113 g), divided

⅓ cup mayonnaise (light or regular)

⅓ cup 14% (full-fat) sour cream

¼ cup buttermilk

1 tbsp white wine vinegar

1 tbsp freshly squeezed lemon juice

1 tsp minced garlic

¼ tsp freshly ground black pepper

Salad

1 medium head iceberg lettuce

6 slices bacon, cooked and chopped

1 cup quartered grape tomatoes

2 tbsp minced fresh chives

Place 3 oz blue cheese plus all remaining dressing ingredients in the bowl of a mini food processor and whirl until almost smooth. The dressing should still have some texture, but no lumps. If you prefer a smoother dressing, keep whirling. Refrigerate dressing until ready to use.

Remove any wilted outer leaves from the lettuce. Cut the lettuce into quarters through its core so that each wedge holds together (see Kitchen Whizdom). Place lettuce wedges on a serving plate. Drizzle generously with dressing and top with remaining 1 oz blue cheese, bacon, tomatoes and chives. Some freshly ground black pepper would be nice, too. Serve immediately.

Note: You may need to thin the dressing with more buttermilk to get the consistency you prefer. This recipe makes more dressing than you'll need. Cover and refrigerate leftovers for up to 3 days.

Makes 4 servings

Per serving: 231 calories, 16 g total fat (7.1 g saturated fat), 12.4 g protein, 9 g carbohydrate (2.8 g fiber, 3.4 g sugars), 36 mg cholesterol, 632 mg sodium

Iceberg lettuce is ideal for wedge salads because it's irresistibly crunchy with its tightly layered leaves. Grab a whole head of iceberg lettuce and cut it in half, from the top down to the stem. Then cut each half again, to make 4 quarters of lettuce. Slice or chop some of the bacon and tomatoes into uniform, little pieces to create edible confetti (well, okay, a bit bigger than confetti!) that you sprinkle over top of the wedges. Small bits will stick to the dressing, while larger pieces can surround the wedge on the plate. See photo for reference. Pretty!

SWAP IT

Use Caesar, Parmesan or ranch dressing instead of blue cheese dressing.

TOP IT

Serve with crushed Sourdough Croutons on page 249.

Classics

The Notable Niçoise Salad

with white wine-shallot vinaigrette

GF DF

Let's take our taste buds on a trip to the south of France, shall we? This stunning, elegant, Julia Child-approved salad takes some time to prepare since it contains many components, but once the beans, potatoes and eggs are cooked, assembly is a snap.

Dressing

⅓ cup olive oil

3 tbsp white wine vinegar

2 tbsp freshly squeezed lemon juice

1 tbsp Dijon mustard

1 tbsp liquid honey

1 tbsp minced shallots

2 tsp minced fresh thyme, or ½ tsp dried thyme

¼ tsp sea salt

⅛ tsp freshly ground black pepper

Salad

12 unpeeled baby potatoes

12 oz (340 g) French (skinny) green beans

1 pkg (5 oz/142 g) mixed greens

2 to 3 cans (6 oz/170 g each) oil-packed tuna, drained

1½ cups halved cherry tomatoes

4 hard-boiled eggs, quartered

½ cup whole olives (your favorite kind)

½ cup very thinly sliced red onions

Whisk together all dressing ingredients in a small bowl or measuring cup. Set aside until ready to use.

Place potatoes in a pot of cold water and bring to a boil. Reduce heat and simmer for 10 to 15 minutes, just until potatoes are fork-tender. Drain potatoes and place them on a cutting board to cool. When cool enough to handle, slice potatoes in half and set aside.

Blanch the beans: While potatoes are simmering, bring a pot of salted water to a boil. Add green beans and cook for 3 minutes. Drain beans and place them in an ice bath to stop the cooking action. Drain again.

Place leafy greens over the bottom of a large, shallow serving bowl (pictured) or rimmed platter. Arrange potatoes, beans and all remaining salad ingredients over greens. Drizzle dressing over salad or serve it on the side. Let your family or guests serve themselves—and pass the pepper grinder!

Makes 6 servings

Per serving: 327 calories, 18.4 g total fat (3.4 g saturated fat), 18.3 g protein, 22.4 g carbohydrate (4.6 g fiber, 9.4 g sugars), 143 mg cholesterol, 433 mg sodium

SWAP IT

Try it with salmon and asparagus instead of tuna and green beans. YUM!

TOP IT

A few thinly sliced radishes add crunch and even more color!

Some assembly required

Broccoli & Bacon Salad

with dried cranberries and sunflower seeds

The original, decades-old recipe for this popular potluck salad was loaded with sugar—very likely the reason I couldn't get enough of it as a child. I've pared back the sugar to 2 tablespoons, which adds the perfect amount of sweetness to balance the tang of the vinegar and lemon juice in the dressing. This crowd-pleasing salad is a treat, a splurge—and worth the occasional indulgence!

Dressing

⅔ cup mayonnaise (light or regular)
⅓ cup 14% (full-fat) sour cream
2 tbsp granulated sugar
1 tbsp apple cider vinegar
1 tbsp freshly squeezed lemon juice
½ tsp celery seed
½ tsp sea salt
⅛ tsp freshly ground black pepper

Salad

6 cups chopped broccoli florets and stems (see Kitchen Whizdom)
6 slices bacon, cooked and chopped
½ cup sweetened dried cranberries
½ cup roasted salted sunflower seeds
½ cup shredded old (sharp) cheddar cheese (2 oz/57 g)
⅓ cup minced red onions

Whisk together all dressing ingredients in a small bowl. Cover and refrigerate until ready to use (up to 1 day in advance).

Combine all salad ingredients in a large bowl. Add dressing and mix well, until ingredients are evenly coated. I use a spatula and turn the salad over and over until everything's well blended. Cover and refrigerate until ready to serve, at least 2 hours for the best flavor.

Makes about 8 cups salad

Per cup: 246 calories, 16.6 g total fat (4.1 g saturated fat), 9 g protein, 18.8 g carbohydrate (2.8 g fiber, 10 g sugars), 18 mg cholesterol, 487 mg sodium

You'll need the equivalent of 1 large head of broccoli for this recipe, but don't use the tough stalk; just chop up the florets and about 2 inches of the stems. Broccoli crowns don't include the stalk, so they're perfect in broccoli salad. Know what else works well? Broccoli slaw mix! It gives the salad a different look and vibe, but it's still super tasty.

SWAP IT

Use toasted, sliced almonds instead of sunflower seeds.

TOP IT

Cook an extra slice of bacon to chop and sprinkle over the salad before serving, along with a few extra cranberries and sunflower seeds.

CHAPTER 6

THE IN-BETWEENS

These outstanding outliers are in a category all by themselves. Literally.

Golden Beet Caprese Salad

with maple-balsamic glaze and toasted pine nuts

When summer's over and tomatoes are no longer in season, my fall/winter roasted root version of the famous Caprese salad can't be beet! It's a showstopping side dish fit for any holiday gathering.

- **4 medium-large golden beets (about 2 lbs/907 g)**
- **⅓ cup balsamic vinegar**
- **1 tbsp pure maple syrup**
- **12 oz (340 g) fresh mozzarella cheese, sliced**
- **1 tbsp olive oil**
- **Sea salt and freshly ground black pepper to taste**
- **Fresh basil leaves**
- **2 tbsp toasted pine nuts**

Start by roasting the beets: Preheat oven to 400°F. I prefer peeling golden beets BEFORE roasting, using a vegetable peeler. So please do that! Wrap the 4 peeled beets loosely with foil, together, but not touching. Place the beet "packet" on a baking sheet and roast the beets until tender, 45 minutes to 75 minutes, depending on their size. You should be able to pierce through the beets with a fork using light pressure. Remove beets from oven and let cool before slicing.

While beets are cooling, make the balsamic glaze: Whisk together balsamic vinegar and maple syrup in your smallest pot or skillet over medium-high heat. When mixture comes to a boil, reduce heat immediately to a gentle simmer. Turn on your vent hood. Simmering vinegar can smell quite strong! Let the mixture simmer (not boil) until it begins to get syrupy and reduces in quantity by about half, whisking occasionally. This should take no more than 5 minutes. It will coat the pan or skillet if you swirl it around. Remove from heat and cool slightly before serving. It'll thicken a bit as it cools, so keep this in mind. If you accidentally thicken it too much, you can thin it with water.

To assemble salad, alternate layers of sliced beets and mozzarella on a serving dish as in photo. Drizzle with olive oil, sprinkle with salt and pepper, then drizzle with 2 tbsp balsamic glaze. Top with fresh basil (either whole leaves or chiffonade cut) and toasted pine nuts. Serve immediately with extra glaze on the side.

Makes 8 side-dish servings

Per serving: 205 calories, 11.6 g total fat (5.3 g saturated fat), 10.1 g protein, 14.6 g carbohydrate (2.7 g fiber, 12.9 g sugars), 28 mg cholesterol, 159 mg sodium

SWAP IT
Try finely chopped pistachios instead of pine nuts.
TOP IT
Add some pomegranate seeds for a pretty holiday presentation.

SUMMER FRESH

Heirloom Tomato Salad

with basil, dill and balsamic vinaigrette

When farmers markets are overflowing with gorgeous tomatoes of all varieties, shapes and sizes, take advantage and buy as many as you can carry! This extra-easy but super-tasty salad benefits from peak ripeness and lightly embellishes the tomatoes with fresh herbs, some crumbled feta and a splish-splash of balsamic dressing.

Dressing

3 tbsp olive oil

2 tbsp balsamic vinegar

1 tbsp minced fresh dill

2 tsp pure maple syrup

1 tsp minced garlic

½ tsp Dijon mustard

¼ tsp sea salt

⅛ tsp freshly ground black pepper

Salad

1½ lbs (680 g) assorted heirloom tomatoes, sliced (see Kitchen Whizdom)

¾ cup crumbled light or regular feta cheese (3 oz/85 g)

½ cup very thinly sliced red onions

⅓ cup torn fresh basil leaves

Sea salt and freshly ground black pepper to taste

Whisk together all dressing ingredients in a small bowl or measuring cup. Set aside.

Arrange sliced tomatoes on a rimmed serving platter. Top with feta and onions. Drizzle generously with dressing, then top with basil and a sprinkle of salt and pepper. Serve immediately. (Do not refrigerate tomato salads—cold temperatures zap their flavor.)

Makes 6 side-dish servings

Per serving: 129 calories, 9.1 g total fat (2.4 g saturated fat), 4.6 g protein, 8.2 g carbohydrate (1.1 g fiber, 5.5 g sugars), 7 mg cholesterol, 284 mg sodium

Despite their name, heirloom tomatoes aren't sold at antique stores but are found at farmers markets and some well-stocked grocery stores. They can be weirdly shaped and oddly colored, yet we prize them for their delicious flavor and appearance despite these idiosyncrasies. Their seeds are what make them heirloom tomatoes. Passed down from season to season, the seeds are taken from tomato plants that produced the best fruit. No science-y, GMO stuff here. Be gentle with your heirlooms, though, since they're generally thin-skinned compared to hybrid tomatoes, making them more likely to bruise. In the photo on the right, you'll notice some colored grape tomatoes, which I thought were a nice addition to the heirlooms.

Fresh from the vine makes
tomatoes divine!
SWAP IT
Use fresh mozzarella
instead of feta. Milder
but magnifico!
TOP IT
If company's coming, I'll throw some
cute sprouts on top, which typically gets
compliments for presentation. ☺

High-Protein Chicken Salad

with lemony Greek-yogurt dressing

I've swapped out most of the mayo in this chunky chicken salad recipe for protein-packed Greek yogurt, creating a creamy-yet-healthy, dill-ightful dressing. Feeling ravenous? Chopped rotisserie chicken, toasted almonds, bright green peas, crunchy celery and diced, hard-boiled eggs will fill you up without weighing you down. Meal prep this salad for lunches or use it as a tasty filling for low-carb lettuce wraps.

Dressing

¾ cup plain 0% Greek yogurt

¼ cup light mayonnaise

2 tbsp minced fresh dill

2 tbsp white vinegar

1 tbsp freshly squeezed lemon juice

1 tbsp liquid honey

1 tbsp Dijon mustard

1 tsp grated lemon zest

½ tsp celery seed (optional)

½ tsp sea salt

¼ tsp freshly ground black pepper

Salad

4 cups chopped rotisserie chicken (light and dark meat)

1½ cups diced celery

1 cup diced red bell peppers

½ cup sliced almonds, lightly toasted

½ cup frozen green peas, thawed

½ cup chopped green onions

¼ cup chopped fresh parsley

4 hard-boiled eggs, chopped

Whisk together all dressing ingredients in a small bowl. Cover and refrigerate until ready to use. For the best flavor, make the dressing 1 day before you need it.

Combine all salad ingredients except eggs in a large bowl. Mix well. Add eggs and dressing and mix again, until all ingredients are well coated with dressing. Refrigerate for at least 1 hour before serving.

Makes about 8 cups salad

Per cup: 220 calories, 8.7 g total fat (1.8 g saturated fat), 27.2 g protein, 8.1 g carbohydrate (2 g fiber, 4.8 g sugars), 156 mg cholesterol, 322 mg sodium

SWAP IT
Try this salad with leftover holiday turkey!
27 GRAMS OF PROTEIN PER CUP
TOP IT
Feel like splurging? "Garnish" the salad with ¼ cup cooked and crumbled bacon before serving.

Mediterranean Hummus Salad

with the fluffiest, uber-creamy hummus

GF DF V

Know what's even better than a classic hummus? A classic hummus topped with a delicious Mediterranean salad! Spoon it onto your dinner plate as a side dish or serve this beautiful salad as an appetizer or snack with fresh pita or naan bread.

Hummus

1 can (19 oz/540 mL) no-salt-added chickpeas, drained and rinsed

½ tsp baking soda

½ cup tahini (I like Soom brand)

3 tbsp freshly squeezed lemon juice

1 tbsp olive oil

2 tsp minced garlic

1 tsp grated lemon zest

½ tsp ground cumin

¾ tsp sea salt

2 to 4 tbsp ice water

Salad

1 cup finely chopped grape tomatoes

1 cup diced mini cucumbers

⅓ cup minced red onions

¼ cup chopped pitted Kalamata olives

¼ cup crumbled light or regular feta cheese (1 oz/28 g; optional)

2 tbsp minced fresh herbs (dill, parsley or mint—or a combination)

Sea salt and freshy ground black pepper to taste

1 tbsp olive oil for drizzling

Place chickpeas in a medium pot and add enough cold water to cover chickpeas by 2 inches. Stir in baking soda. Bring to a boil over high heat. Reduce heat to low and simmer, uncovered, for 15 minutes.

While chickpeas are simmering, combine all salad ingredients in a medium bowl and mix well. Set aside.

Drain chickpeas in a mesh sieve and rinse well with cold water. Don't discard the skins! Place chickpeas (with skins) and all remaining hummus ingredients, except water, into the bowl of a 7-cup food processor. Whirl for 2 full minutes. Mixture will be thick. Add 2 tbsp ice water and whirl again for 20 seconds. If you prefer thinner hummus, add more ice water by the spoonful until you're happy with the texture.

Spoon the hummus onto a 10-inch, rimmed plate, spreading it out with a raised edge. Mound the vegetable mixture on the hummus, leaving half or one-third of the hummus visible. Drizzle olive oil over the salad and hummus and serve at room temperature.

Makes 6 to 8 servings

Per serving (based on 8 servings): 206 calories, 12.6 g total fat (1.8 g saturated fat), 6.8 g protein, 17 g carbohydrate (5 g fiber, 1.3 g sugars), 0 mg cholesterol, 326 mg sodium

SWAP IT

Use white kidney beans (cannellini) instead of chickpeas (no simmering required).

TOP IT

Sprinkle a light dusting of paprika over the hummus before serving.

Shrimp, Mango & Avocado Salad

with honey-lime dressing

This fresh and fabulous salad screams "summertime!"—but you'll want to eat it all year round. It's impressive, yet quite simple to make as a light lunch or stunning side dish. I eat this salad with a spoon, since it does a better job of acting like a shovel than if I used a fork.

Dressing

2 tbsp olive oil

2 tbsp freshly squeezed lime juice

2 tsp liquid honey

1 tsp Dijon mustard

½ tsp grated lime zest

¼ tsp each sea salt and freshly ground black pepper

⅛ tsp each ground cumin and chili powder (or more to taste)

Salad

1 lb (454 g) jumbo cooked shrimp (about 15 to 20 per pound), chopped (see Kitchen Whizdom)

2 medium mangoes, diced or cubed

1 large or 2 small avocados, diced or cubed

1 cup peeled, diced English cucumbers

1 cup quartered grape tomatoes

½ cup very thinly sliced or minced red onions

¼ cup to ⅓ cup chopped fresh cilantro

1 jalapeño pepper, seeded and minced

Small handful of baby arugula just for fun (optional)

Whisk together all dressing ingredients in a small bowl or measuring cup until well blended. Set aside until ready to use.

Combine all salad ingredients in a large bowl. Add the dressing and mix gently, until all ingredients are well coated. Serve immediately.

Makes about 7 cups salad

Per cup: 199 calories, 9.1 g total fat (1.2 g saturated fat), 13 g protein, 18 g carbohydrate (4 g fiber, 11.6 g sugars), 66 mg cholesterol, 269 mg sodium

This pretty salad looks more appealing when you buy jumbo shrimp and coarsely chop them versus using baby shrimp (please don't!). Bonus: You'll get a taste of shrimp in every single bite! See photo for size reference. Make sure your mangoes and avocados are ripe so their flavors shine through. Finally, don't prepare the salad too far in advance, since avocados turn brown very quickly. The fresher the salad, the better!

SWAP IT

When peaches are in season, use them instead of mangoes.

TOP IT

Save some chopped cilantro to sprinkle over the salad just before serving.

Southwestern Grilled Corn Salad

with cherry tomatoes, fresh cilantro and jalapeño

This crisp, colorful and impossibly delicious salad was rated 11/10 by my always-willing taste-tester and neighbor, Mary. Serve it at your next backyard cookout and expect an empty bowl at the end of the gathering. It pairs well with grilled anything: beef, pork, chicken, shrimp or portobello mushrooms.

8 medium cobs fresh corn, shucked

1 medium red bell pepper, seeded and halved

3 tbsp olive oil, divided

1½ cups halved cherry tomatoes

⅓ cup thinly sliced red onions

3 tbsp minced fresh cilantro

1 jalapeño pepper, seeded and minced

2 tbsp freshly squeezed lime juice

½ tsp each ground cumin and chili powder

¼ tsp each sea salt and freshly ground black pepper

Preheat grill to medium-high heat. Brush corn and bell pepper halves lightly with 1 tbsp olive oil. Place corn and bell peppers directly on the grill. Make sure the cobs are resting between the grates to avoid a cob-rolling situation. Close lid.

Grill corn until char marks appear and corn is tender, rotating corn every 2 to 3 minutes. Flip the bell peppers halfway through cooking time. Total cooking time will be 10 to 12 minutes. Be careful not to burn the vegetables. (Note: There are a dozen ways to grill corn, including blanching it for a couple minutes first, then grilling just for grill marks, but this method is simpler and faster. The blanching/grilling method works great if you don't mind the extra time.)

Remove corn and bell peppers from heat. When corn is cool enough to handle, slice the kernels off the cob and place them in a large bowl. Chop the bell pepper halves into bite-sized pieces. Add them to bowl along with all remaining ingredients. Mix well. Serve immediately or cover and refrigerate until serving time.

Makes about 6 cups salad

Per cup: 141 calories, 6.4 g total fat (0.9 g saturated fat), 3.7 g protein, 20.8 g carbohydrate (3 g fiber, 5.8 g sugars), 0 mg cholesterol, 76 mg sodium

SWAP IT

Looks gorgeous with multi-colored cherry or grape tomatoes.

TOP IT

Add grilled shrimp, diced avocados and some black beans for a sensational summertime meal.

Roasted Cauliflower Salad

with dates, pine nuts and fresh herbs

This unique and tasty side-dish salad has cozy fall comfort food written all over it. The sweet, sticky dates and buttery pine nuts complement the roasted cauliflower beautifully, then everything gets tossed in a light dressing with hints of lemon and tahini. Swoon!

Salad

8 cups cauliflower florets*

1 medium red onion, cut into 6 wedges

2 tbsp olive oil

1 tsp ground cumin

½ tsp smoked paprika

½ tsp each sea salt and freshly ground black pepper

½ cup chopped Medjool dates

½ cup toasted pine nuts

¼ cup chopped fresh cilantro

¼ cup chopped fresh parsley

Dressing

2 tbsp olive oil

2 tbsp freshly squeezed lemon juice

1 tbsp tahini

1 tbsp white balsamic vinegar

2 tsp pure maple syrup

½ tsp grated lemon zest

¼ tsp each sea salt and freshly ground black pepper

***From 1 very large head of cauliflower or 2 small heads.**

Preheat oven to 400°F. Arrange cauliflower florets and onion wedges in a single layer on a large nonstick rimmed baking sheet. Drizzle with olive oil and sprinkle with cumin, paprika, salt and pepper. Use your hands to evenly coat the vegetables with seasonings.

Roast cauliflower and onions for about 25 minutes, stirring once halfway through cooking time. Cauliflower should be tender and browned around the edges. Remove from oven and let cool. Chop onions into smaller pieces and place the cauliflower and onions in a large bowl.

Whisk together all dressing ingredients in a small bowl or measuring cup. Add dates, pine nuts, herbs and dressing to cauliflower-onion mixture. Toss or stir gently to combine. Serve warm or at room temperature.

Makes 6 to 8 side-dish servings

Per serving (based on 8 servings): 186 calories, 13.7 g total fat (1.6 g saturated fat), 3.7 g protein, 14.2 g carbohydrate (3.3 g fiber, 8.6 g sugars), 0 mg cholesterol, 248 mg sodium

Chopped dates
TASTE GREAT!
SWAP IT
Use toasted, slivered almonds instead of pine nuts and chopped raisins instead of dates.
TOP IT
If serving this dish during the holidays, throw a few pomegranate seeds on top for added sparkle.

Sweet Beet & Balsamic Salad

with cranberries, caramelized pecans and feta

I created this recipe for my dear friend, Jackie, who I'd describe as a sweet person who loves sweet salads. Truthfully, Jackie loves sweet "anything," and once fed me a dinner buffet of chocolate-covered almonds, jelly beans and marshmallows, followed by chocolate-dipped strawberries for dessert. This salad ticks all the boxes for Jackie: flavor, texture, color and sweetness, with a bit of salty feta thrown in for contrast.

Salad

4 large beets (about 2½ lbs/1.13 kg), scrubbed clean (see Kitchen Whizdom)

1 tbsp olive oil

Sea salt and freshly ground black pepper

Big handful baby arugula

½ cup caramelized pecan halves, chopped (see recipe, page 253)

½ cup crumbled light or regular feta cheese (2 oz/57 g)

⅓ cup sweetened dried cranberries

Dressing

3 tbsp olive oil

2 tbsp balsamic vinegar

1 tbsp light mayonnaise

2 tsp liquid honey

1 tsp Dijon mustard

¼ tsp sea salt

⅛ tsp freshly ground black pepper

Preheat oven to 400°F. Line a medium rimmed baking sheet with parchment paper for easy cleanup. Set aside.

Trim the ends from beets to create a flat surface, then cut them into ¾-inch cubes/pieces. Don't get out your measuring tape—the goal is to create uniform pieces for even roasting. Place chopped beets on the baking sheet, drizzle with olive oil and sprinkle lightly with salt and pepper. Mix well to evenly coat with seasonings (using your gloved hands).

Roast beets for 35 to 40 minutes or until fork-tender, stirring once halfway through cooking time. While beets are roasting, make the dressing: Whisk together all dressing ingredients in a small bowl or measuring cup. Set aside.

Remove beets from oven and let cool slightly. They're hot! To assemble salad, place arugula in a large serving bowl and top with beets, pecans, feta and cranberries. Drizzle dressing over salad. Toss and serve immediately.

Makes 8 side-dish servings

Per serving: 206 calories, 10.7 g total fat (1.9 g saturated fat), 4.6 g protein, 25 g carbohydrate (5 g fiber, 19 g sugars), 4 mg cholesterol, 296 mg sodium

Beet skins are edible, just like the skins on potatoes. If you scrub the beets well, there's no need to peel them. Yay! I scrub them under running water using an abrasive kitchen sponge that I dedicate exclusively for this purpose. I find this works even better than a vegetable scrubber brush. Always wear gloves, since handling red beets can stain your fingers.

SWAP IT
Try this salad with roasted sweet potatoes instead of beets. Wowzers!
UN-BEET-ABLE flavor!
TOP IT
Sprinkle with 1 tbsp minced parsley for a pop of freshness.

Herb Your Enthusiasm

My top 5 picks for mint-condition salads

BASIL

Summer in a leaf! Sweet, almost minty, slightly peppery.

DILL

Delicate, feathery, subtle sweetness, kinda grassy in the best way.

CILANTRO

Citrusy, peppery, pungent, perfect!

PARSLEY

(CURLY AND ITALIAN)

Curly: Fluffy, sturdy leaves, milder flavor.
Italian: Broad, flat leaves, stronger flavor.

MINT

Sweet and herbal, cool and refreshing!

Fresh herbs can take a salad from simple to sensational by adding a touch of garden-fresh magic.

Turkey, Cranberry & Pecan Salad

with chopped apple and orange-yogurt dressing

I'd normally make this deliciously crunchy, high-protein salad with leftover Thanksgiving turkey, but it's gobble-icious any time of year, since the ingredients are easy to find and the recipe is pretty simple. For workday lunch or in a wrap, you'll make this salad in a snap!

Dressing

½ cup plain 0% Greek yogurt

¼ cup light mayonnaise

2 tbsp frozen orange juice concentrate, thawed

2 tsp honey mustard

1 tsp white vinegar

¼ tsp sea salt

⅛ tsp freshly ground black pepper

Salad

4 cups chopped cooked turkey breast

1 cup diced celery (see Kitchen Whizdom)

1 large Gala apple, unpeeled, diced

½ cup chopped pecans, lightly toasted

½ cup sweetened dried cranberries

⅓ cup chopped green onions

⅓ cup chopped fresh parsley

Whisk together all dressing ingredients in a small bowl. Cover and refrigerate until ready to use.

Combine all salad ingredients in a large bowl. Add dressing and mix again, until all ingredients are well coated. Chill for 1 hour before serving.

Makes about 7 cups salad

Per cup: 215 calories, 8.9 g total fat (1 g saturated fat), 21 g protein, 14.7 g carbohydrate (2.1 g fiber, 10 g sugars), 48 mg cholesterol, 294 mg sodium

Celery finds its way into a surprising number of salads, since it adds texture, color, freshness and crunch without overwhelming flavor. I'm somewhat obsessive about the way I chop celery (shocking, I know) and, for some bizarro reason, I don't like celery cut into the standard U-shape. My method: Wash celery stalk, trim off both ends, cut celery stalk in half crosswise, cut the two halves lengthwise to get 4 long pieces, gather the 4 pieces and dice with your sharpest knife. Ta-da! Uniform dices, no U-shapes, no celery anxiety. Phew!

SWITCH IT UP

Use chopped chicken breasts instead of turkey and walnuts instead of pecans.

JAZZ IT UP

Add ½ tsp poppy seeds to the dressing.

Strawberry & Watermelon Salad

with cucumbers, feta and mint

Sometimes simple can be simply amazing! Crisp, cool and refreshing watermelon pairs perfectly with juicy strawberries and tangy lime juice. Chunks of feta and sprigs of fresh mint take it over the top. Serve this vibrant salad on a hot summer day.

Salad

3 cups sliced or chopped strawberries

3 cups cubed seedless watermelon

1 cup diced or sliced English cucumbers

½ cup very thinly sliced red onions

⅓ cup chopped fresh mint

1 cup diced or crumbled light or regular feta cheese (4 oz/113 g)

Dressing

2 tbsp olive oil

2 tbsp freshly squeezed lime juice

1 tbsp liquid honey

½ tsp grated lime zest

¼ tsp each sea salt and freshly ground black pepper

In a large bowl, combine all salad ingredients except feta. Mix gently.

Whisk together all dressing ingredients in a small bowl or measuring cup. Pour over salad. Mix gently to coat salad with dressing. Add feta and mix again. Serve immediately.

Makes about 8 cups salad

Per cup: 112 calories, 5.7 g total fat (1.8 g saturated fat), 4 g protein, 14 g carbohydrate (2.3 g fiber, 9 g sugars), 5 mg cholesterol, 272 mg sodium

This pretty salad makes a deliciously fresh sidekick to grilled salmon or chicken. To change things up, try it with mini bocconcini and fresh basil instead of feta and mint. If making the bocconcini-basil version, add 1 tsp balsamic vinegar to the dressing. For a vegan salad, use pure maple syrup instead of honey, leave out the feta and add 1 cup diced avocados just before serving.

EASY AND
summer
BREEZY!

Fresh & Fabulous Fruit Salad

for holiday brunches or anytime lunches

Bursting with color and flavor, this spectacular fruit salad always gets rave reviews! Simply dressed with a combo of honey, lime juice and poppy seeds and tossed with fresh mint, you'll dazzle your family during the holidays or any day! Sure, it requires a bit of chopping, but it's quite easy to make, leaving you plenty of time to enjoy the "fruits" of your labor. (Psst! It also makes a striking summer BBQ side dish.)

Salad

2 cups diced mangoes (see Kitchen Whizdom)

2 cups fresh blueberries

2 cups seedless mandarin orange segments (not canned)

2 cups halved seedless red grapes

2 cups peeled diced kiwi fruit

2 cups thinly sliced red apple variety like Gala, Red Delicious or Fuji

1 cup pomegranate seeds

¼ cup chopped fresh mint

Dressing

¼ cup freshly squeezed lime juice

2 tbsp liquid honey

1 tsp grated lime zest

1 tsp poppy seeds

Combine all salad ingredients in a large bowl and set aside.

Make the dressing: Whisk together all dressing ingredients in a small bowl or measuring cup. Pour over salad and stir gently to avoid squishing the fruit. Serve immediately or cover and chill for up to 2 hours before serving. If making ahead, stir in the mint just before serving.

Makes about 13 cups salad

Per cup: 112 calories, 0.7 g total fat (0 g saturated fat), 1.5 g protein, 27 g carbohydrate (3.8 g fiber, 21 g sugars), 0 mg cholesterol, 3 mg sodium

When shopping for mangoes, kiwis, peaches, nectarines, papayas and avocados, just remember the old Supertramp strong, "Give a Little Bit." A ripe mango will be slightly soft and "give a little bit" when pressed with your thumb or gently squeezed. If it's hard, it's not ripe and will have very little flavor. An underripe kiwi will feel stiff and firm with almost no give, sorta like squeezing an apple. I'm stating the obvious here, but a fabulous fruit salad needs ripe, delicious fruits! Singing and pressing in the produce aisle means you won't need to "Take the Long Way Home" while your fruits ripen.

SUNSHINE in a BOWL
SWITCH IT UP
Vary the fruits based on what's in season. In the summer, use diced strawberries instead of pomegranate.
JAZZ IT UP
Top individual servings with a dollop of vanilla Greek yogurt.

COOL & CRISP

Mini Cucumber Salad

with chickpeas, feta and dill

GF

Could it get any easier? Combine four main ingredients (cucumbers, chickpeas, red onions, feta cheese), one fresh herb (dill) and a simple, red wine vinaigrette—and voilà! A fresh and flavorful, fuss-free salad you'll have on repeat all year round. It's perfect for potlucks, summer parties and holiday gatherings.

Salad

5 cups sliced mini (Persian) cucumbers (see Kitchen Whizdom)

1 can (19 oz/540 mL) no-salt-added chickpeas, drained and rinsed

1 cup crumbled light or regular feta cheese (4 oz/113 g)

½ cup minced red onions

3 tbsp minced fresh dill

Dressing

3 tbsp olive oil

2 tbsp red wine vinegar

1 tbsp freshly squeezed lemon juice

2 tsp liquid honey

1 tsp Dijon mustard

1 tsp minced garlic

¼ tsp sea salt

⅛ tsp freshly ground black pepper

Combine all salad ingredients in a large bowl and set aside.

Whisk together all dressing ingredients in a small bowl or measuring cup until well blended. Pour over salad and stir gently until all ingredients are coated with dressing. Top with a few grinds of black pepper and serve immediately, or cover and refrigerate until ready to serve.

Makes about 8 cups salad

Per cup: 160 calories, 8.4 g total fat (2.3 saturated fat), 7.4 g protein, 15 g carbohydrate (2.7 g fiber, 3 g sugars), 7 mg cholesterol, 260 mg sodium

Persian cucumbers are those cute, little guys sold in packages of 5 or 6 and labeled "mini cucumbers." They're 5 to 6 inches long, narrow and have teeny, tiny seeds, so they won't make your salad watery. You'll need about 8 mini cucumbers for this recipe. English cucumbers are a good substitute—just slice them into rounds then cut each round in half. For the feta cheese, I always buy a block and crumble it myself, since pre-crumbled feta is too powdery and dry for my taste.

SWAP IT

Not a fan of dill?
Try parsley or cilantro.

TOP IT

Add 1 cup diced avocados
just before serving.

CHOP-CHOP Beet & Apple Salad

with lemony balsamic dressing

GF DF V

I love combining earthy, savory and sweet flavors in salads—and this vibrant beet, apple, cabbage, carrot, pomegranate and herb medley is a healthy, crunchy, texture-filled case in point! Plus, any salad that requires seven commas to describe it is worth making, don't you think? For convenience, I use precooked, vacuum-packed beets—peeled and ready to eat. Sweet!

Salad

2 cups diced cooked carrots (see Kitchen Whizdom)

2 cups chopped red cabbage

2 cups unpeeled diced apples (I use Red Delicious; see Kitchen Whizdom)

2 cups diced cooked beets

1 cup pomegranate seeds

½ cup chopped fresh parsley

⅓ cup minced red onions

2 tbsp minced fresh dill

Dressing

⅓ cup olive oil

2 tbsp freshly squeezed lemon juice

2 tbsp white balsamic vinegar

1 tbsp pure maple syrup

2 tsp Dijon mustard

¼ tsp sea salt

⅛ tsp freshly ground black pepper

Do your best to chop the carrots, cabbage, apples and beets into pieces of similar size. I always wear latex gloves when slicing beets to avoid staining my hands and/or ruining my manicure. ☺

Combine all salad ingredients, except beets, in a large mixing bowl. Mix well and set aside.

Make the dressing: Whisk together all dressing ingredients in a small bowl or measuring cup. Pour dressing over salad and mix well. Add the beets and mix again. The beets will stain the other vegetables so it's best to add them last, just before serving.

Makes about 9 cups salad

Per cup: 148 calories, 8.6 g total fat (1.2 g saturated fat), 1.4 g protein, 17.6 g carbohydrate (4.1 g fiber, 12 g sugars), 0 mg cholesterol, 151 mg sodium

Wondering why I'm using cooked carrots in this salad? Thought so! Diced raw carrots are just too hard, crunchy and somewhat annoying, to be honest. So, the options are (1) grate the carrots or (2) cook the carrots. Grated carrots make this salad look messy and disheveled and that hurts my brain. Steaming or boiling the carrots until *al dente* (as if you're cooking pasta) is the way to go. For simplicity, use baby carrots, steam or boil them until almost tender, let them cool, slice them lengthwise and then dice into uniform pieces. Not too little, not too big. Perfect! Also, diced apples turn brown quickly, so it helps to toss them in some lemon juice while prepping the other salad ingredients.

SWAP IT

Use apple cider vinegar instead of white balsamic. It has a stronger flavor but works well in this recipe.

TOP IT

Crumbled feta or blue cheese would be tasty! Sprinkle it on individual servings.

Halloumi, Watermelon & Avocado Salad

with fresh mint and balsamic glaze

All hail halloumi, the Cypriot cheese sensation that can be grilled or pan-fried without melting! I was introduced to this salty, squeaky, highly addictive cheese years ago by my friends Jackie and Alex. Alex's mother, Georgia, would import (smuggle) giant jars of authentic, straight-from-the-homeland, mint-marinated halloumi into Canada, and we'd all line up (fight) to get a taste of it. I mean, it's a cheese you can actually grill—and it doesn't melt! Miraculous! And paired with watermelon? Oh my goodness, it's wonderful.

Marinated Halloumi

1 pkg (9 oz/250 g) halloumi cheese

2 tbsp olive oil

1 tbsp freshly squeezed lemon juice

½ tsp grated lemon zest

½ tsp each dried oregano and dried thyme

¼ tsp freshly ground black pepper

Salad

¼ large seedless watermelon, sliced into triangles

1 large avocado, sliced

⅓ cup very thinly sliced red onions

1 tbsp freshly squeezed lemon juice

1 to 2 tbsp balsamic glaze (see recipe, page 172)

Freshly ground black pepper to taste

10 fresh mint leaves, torn or chopped

Slice halloumi into ¼-inch-thick slices and arrange them on a dinner plate in a single layer. In a small bowl, whisk together olive oil, lemon juice and zest, oregano, thyme and pepper. Brush marinade over both sides of halloumi slices. Cover and refrigerate for 2 hours.

Arrange watermelon, avocado and red onions on a serving platter. Sprinkle lemon juice over the avocado to delay browning. Set aside.

Heat a grill pan (or nonstick skillet) over medium-high heat. Place the marinated halloumi slices on the grill pan and cook on each side for 2 to 3 minutes, or until nice grill marks form and the cheese has softened.

Quickly add the warm halloumi to the platter and drizzle balsamic glaze over all ingredients. Top with freshly ground black pepper and mint. Serve immediately.

Makes 6 side-dish servings

Per serving: 240 calories, 17 g total fat (7.6 g saturated fat), 10.6 g protein, 12 g carbohydrate (2.8 g fiber, 6.9 g sugars), 33 mg cholesterol, 487 mg sodium

SWAP IT

Replace the fresh mint with basil or use a bit of both.

TOP IT

Sprinkle 2 tbsp chopped pistachios or toasted pine nuts over the salad before serving.

Spring Roll Salad Bowl

with colorful veggies, shrimp and peanut dressing

No more fussing with sticky, finicky rice paper wraps when you're craving Vietnamese-style fresh spring rolls! This fully loaded, deconstructed version needs some prep (chopping!), but then it comes together quickly. The flavor-packed peanut sauce is the boss!

Dressing/Sauce

½ cup natural peanut butter

2 tbsp reduced-sodium soy sauce (use tamari soy sauce for gluten-free)

2 tbsp seasoned rice vinegar

2 tbsp freshly squeezed lime juice

2 tbsp liquid honey

1 tbsp dark sesame oil

1 tbsp grated fresh gingerroot

2 tsp minced garlic

1 tsp Sriracha hot sauce

2 to 4 tbsp warm water

Salad

6 oz (170 g) uncooked rice vermicelli noodles

1 lb (454 g) jumbo cooked shrimp (whole or chopped)

1 small English cucumber, cut into matchsticks

1 medium red bell pepper, cut into matchsticks

1 medium mango, diced or sliced

1 cup grated carrots

1 cup very thinly sliced red cabbage

1 cup chopped romaine lettuce

½ cup chopped green onions

⅓ cup chopped fresh cilantro

⅓ cup chopped peanuts

Whirl together all dressing ingredients in a small blender or food processor until smooth and creamy. Add warm water as needed to reach desired consistency. Set aside until ready to use.

Cook vermicelli according to package directions. Drain and rinse with cold water. Drain again. Transfer cooked noodles to a large mixing bowl and use kitchen shears to snip the noodles a few times.

Add all remaining salad ingredients except peanuts to noodles. Mix well using tongs. Add ¾ cup dressing and mix again. This may be enough dressing for you. Feel free to add all the dressing if you like it saucy! Garnish individual servings with chopped peanuts. Serve immediately.

Note: Leftover dressing can be stored in the fridge for up to 4 days.

Makes 4 servings

Per serving: 520 calories, 18.8 g total fat (2.7 g saturated fat), 32 g protein, 57.5 g carbohydrate (6.7 g fiber, 20 g sugars), 116 mg cholesterol, 682 mg sodium

SWITCH IT UP

Use chopped rotisserie chicken instead of shrimp.

JAZZ IT UP

Add ¼ cup chopped fresh mint to the salad and sprinkle with toasted sesame seeds before serving.

Steak, Tomato & Avocado Salad

with a fresh and tangy chimichurri-like sauce

If you're of Argentinian or Uruguayan descent, please avert your eyes and skip on over to the next recipe, since I'm about to tinker with your beloved chimichurri sauce! Let's just call my version "chimichurrski," the Podleski twist on traditional chimichurri. It's slightly different, but still mega-herby and delicious, and perfectly complements grilled steak, creamy avocados and juicy tomatoes.

Salad

1½ lbs (680 g) striploin (or your favorite) steak

1 tbsp olive oil

1 tsp steak spice/seasoning (see Kitchen Whizdom)

2 to 3 medium tomatoes, sliced or chopped (see Kitchen Whizdom)

2 medium avocados, sliced or diced

⅓ cup very thinly sliced red onions (optional)

Chimichurri

⅓ cup olive oil

2 tbsp red wine vinegar

2 tbsp finely minced shallots

1 tbsp freshly squeezed lemon juice

2 tsp minced garlic

1 tsp granulated sugar (optional)

½ tsp sea salt

¼ tsp crushed red pepper flakes

½ cup finely chopped fresh flat-leaf parsley

¼ cup finely chopped fresh cilantro

Rub the steaks on both sides with olive oil. Sprinkle with steak spice and rub it in. Let steaks sit at room temperature for 20 minutes while you preheat the grill to medium-high heat.

While grill is heating up, make the chimichurri: In a small bowl, whisk together olive oil through to red pepper flakes. Stir in parsley and cilantro. Set aside until ready to use.

Lightly oil grill racks. Grill steaks for about 4 minutes per side (with lid down), or to your desired degree of doneness. Be careful not to overcook steaks. Exact grilling time will depend on thickness of steaks. Remove steaks from grill and let them rest while you slice the tomatoes and avocados.

Slice steak thinly and arrange on a serving platter with avocados, tomatoes and red onions, if using. Spoon chimichurri generously over entire salad. Serve immediately with extra sauce on the side.

Makes 4 servings

Per serving: 539 calories, 39 g total fat (7.8 g saturated fat), 38.3 g protein, 10 g carbohydrate (5.1 g fiber, 2.6 g sugars), 99 mg cholesterol, 608 mg sodium

A great addition to any spice rack, dry steak seasoning is sold under various brands at any well-stocked supermarket. The simple combination of garlic, onion, salt, pepper, paprika and mustard gives a nice flavor boost to grilled meats—especially steak. For the tomatoes, use on-the-vine, heirloom or cherry tomatoes.

SWITCH IT UP

Use balsamic vinegar instead of red wine vinegar. So good!

JAZZ IT UP

Grill 2 cobs of fresh corn along with the steaks, slice off the kernels and add them to the salad. Drool.

DIY Taco Salad Bar

with all the fabulous fixings

Spice things up on Taco Tuesday with a build-your-own salad bar featuring the most popular taco toppings! Arranging the ingredients buffet style means each family member or guest can create his or her own custom salad. Let's give 'em something to taco 'bout!

Sour-Cream Topping

1¼ cups light (5%) sour cream

2 tbsp taco seasoning (store-bought or homemade)

2 tbsp freshly squeezed lime juice

1 tsp grated lime zest

1 tsp liquid honey (optional)

Taco Beef

1 tbsp olive oil

1½ lbs (680 g) extra-lean ground beef

1 cup diced onions

2 tsp minced garlic

⅓ cup ketchup

¼ cup water

2 tbsp taco seasoning

For the Salad Bar

1 large head iceberg lettuce, chopped

1½ cups quartered grape tomatoes

1½ cups canned black beans, drained and rinsed

1 can (12 oz/340 mL) whole-kernel corn, drained

1½ cups guacamole

1½ cups salsa

1½ cups shredded old (sharp) cheddar cheese (6 oz/180 g)

½ cup chopped green onions

½ cup chopped fresh cilantro

Combine all sour-cream topping ingredients in a small bowl and mix well. Cover and refrigerate until ready to serve. Prepare this up to one day in advance.

Heat olive oil in a large nonstick skillet over medium-high heat. Add beef, onions and garlic. Cook and stir until beef is no longer pink, breaking up any large pieces. Add ketchup, water and taco seasoning. Mix well and cook for 2 more minutes. Remove skillet from heat and keep warm.

Set up your taco station with all the fixings, including the sour-cream topping. Add the warm beef mixture at the last minute. Serving it in the skillet (sitting on a trivet or tea towel) helps keep the beef warm. Enjoy!

Note: If you prefer a thinner, more traditional salad dressing versus my thicker sour-cream topping, mix 1 cup ranch dressing with 2 tbsp smoky barbecue sauce. So tasty!

Makes 4 to 6 servings

Per serving: All the choices in this DIY Taco Salad Bar make it difficult to calculate nutritional numbers. Are you loading up on guac? Skipping the cheese? Going all-in on the beef? I can't predict how much of each topping you'll consume, but just know this: It's going to be delicious!

Roasted Sweet Potato & Brussels Sprout Salad

with maple-Dijon dressing

An impressive salad for your Thanksgiving dinner table, this fall-like, harvesty beauty is chock-full of flavor with roasted veggies and a delectable, drinkable dressing. Sweet potatoes and Brussels sprouts are meant to be together, like wine and cheese, bread and butter, Ross and Rachel.

Salad

4 cups peeled, cubed sweet potatoes (¾-inch cubes)

1 lb (454 g) Brussels sprouts, halved or quartered (depending on size)

1 medium red onion, cut into 6 wedges

2 tbsp olive oil

1 tsp each paprika, ground cumin and dried thyme

½ tsp sea salt

¼ tsp freshly ground black pepper

Big handful baby arugula or mixed greens

½ cup roasted salted pumpkin seeds

½ cup pomegranate seeds

¾ cup crumbled light or regular feta cheese (3 oz/85 g)

Dressing

¼ cup olive oil

3 tbsp apple cider vinegar

2 tbsp pure maple syrup

1 tbsp Dijon mustard

¼ tsp sea salt

⅛ tsp freshly ground black pepper

Preheat oven to 400°F.

In a very large mixing bowl, combine sweet potatoes, Brussels sprouts and onion. Drizzle with olive oil and toss until well coated. Sprinkle with paprika, cumin, thyme, salt and pepper. Toss again until seasonings are evenly distributed. Spread vegetables in a single layer on a large nonstick rimmed baking sheet. Roast for 20 minutes. Remove veggies from oven, give them a stir, then roast for another 10 to 15 minutes, until tender, depending on their size. Be careful not to burn them. Remove from oven and let cool slightly.

While vegetables are roasting, make the dressing: Whisk together all dressing ingredients in a small bowl or measuring cup until well blended. Set aside.

Add arugula to a large serving bowl and top with roasted vegetables, pumpkin seeds, pomegranate seeds and feta. Drizzle dressing over salad and toss or mix well. Serve immediately.

Makes 8 side-dish servings

Per serving: 275 calories, 16 g total fat (3.2 g saturated fat), 8.3 g protein, 26.6 g carbohydrate (6 g fiber, 9.6 g sugars), 5 mg cholesterol, 420 mg sodium

SWAP IT

Create a filling vegan meal by using warm lentils instead of feta cheese.

TOP IT

Sprinkle with a chopped fresh herb like parsley, dill or cilantro.

Asian Cucumber Salad

with a simple, sweet-and-tangy dressing

 DF 

Cool, crunchy and refreshing, this lightly dressed but highly flavored salad is a cucumber-lover's dream and can be made in under 15 minutes. It's a variation of the Japanese Sunomono salad, which means "vinegared things." I'd pair this delicious and somewhat addictive "vinegared thing" with any Asian-inspired main dish.

6 cups very thinly sliced English cucumbers (see Kitchen Whizdom)

½ tsp sea salt

3 tbsp seasoned rice vinegar

1 tbsp reduced-sodium soy sauce (use tamari soy sauce for gluten-free)

1 tbsp granulated sugar

1 tbsp dark sesame oil

2 tsp grated fresh gingerroot

1 tsp minced garlic

⅛ to ¼ tsp crushed red pepper flakes

2 tbsp thinly sliced green onions

1 tbsp toasted sesame seeds

Toss together cucumber slices and salt in a colander and set it in the sink to drain for 20 minutes. Let osmosis do its job of drawing out moisture from the cucumbers while you make the dressing.

Whisk together vinegar, soy sauce, sugar, sesame oil, gingerroot, garlic and crushed red pepper flakes in a small bowl or measuring cup. Set aside.

Place the salted cucumber slices on several layers of paper towels and squeeze or pat them dry. Add them to a mixing bowl.

Pour dressing over cucumbers and mix well. Sprinkle with green onions and sesame seeds and serve immediately.

Makes about 5 cups salad

Per cup: 84 calories, 4.9 g total fat (0.8 g saturated fat), 1.9 g protein, 9.1 g carbohydrate (1.1 g fiber, 5.4 g sugars), 0 mg cholesterol, 405 mg sodium

Use thin-skinned cucumbers such as English or mini (Persian) cucumbers since they have fewer seeds. Scoring the cucumbers lengthwise with the tines of a fork before slicing them allows the dressing to cling better. It also makes them look pretty—notice the slightly curvy edges of my cucumber slices in the photo? If you own a mandoline slicer with a hand guard, you can slice the cucumbers evenly and quickly. Salting the cucumbers draws out moisture, so the dressing doesn't get too watered down, but you can skip this step if you're cutting back on sodium.

SUPER easy, SUPER tasty!

CHAPTER 7

THE EMBELLISHMENTS

Edible exclamation points, salad toppers and protein boosters.

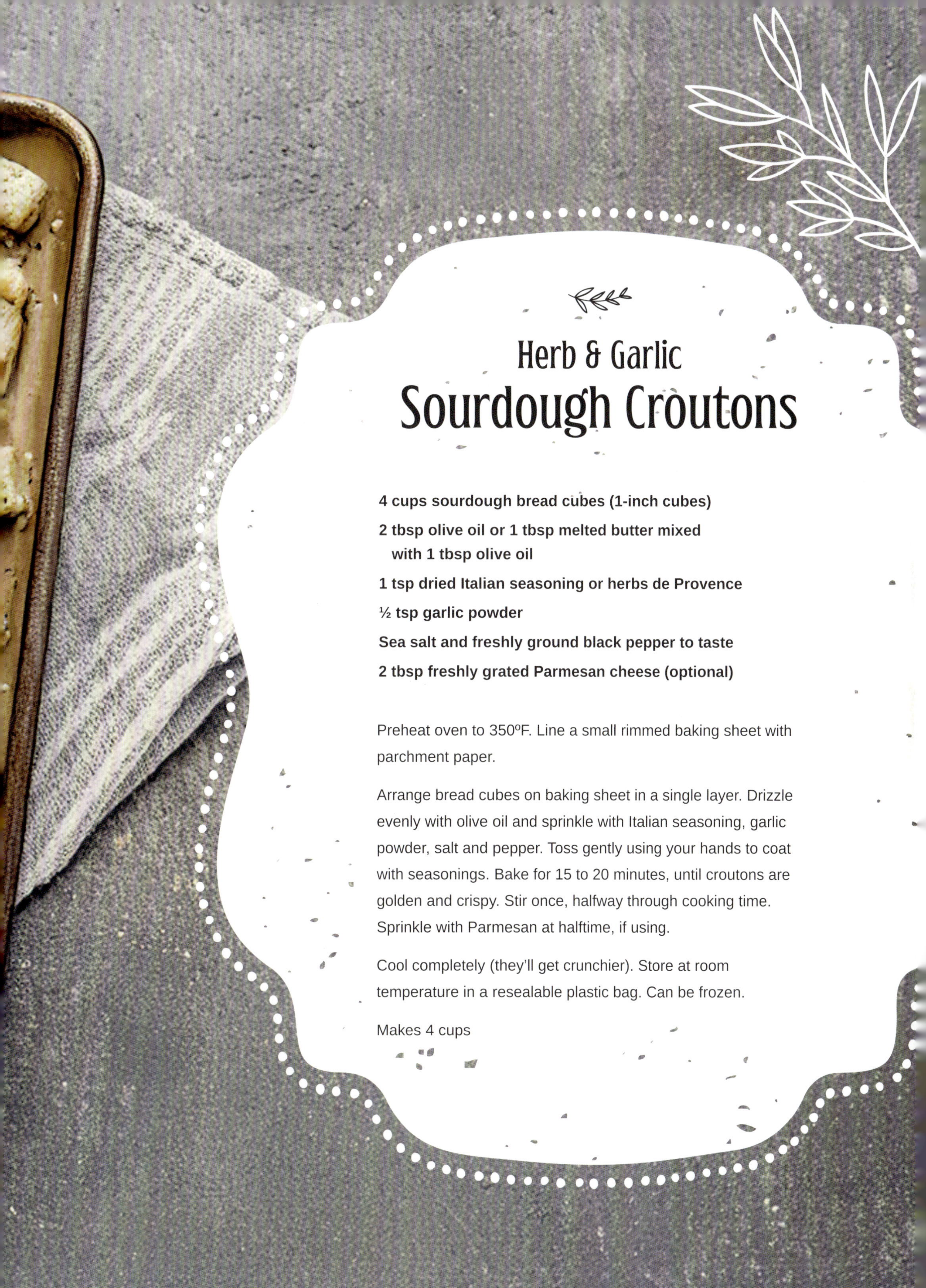

Herb & Garlic
Sourdough Croutons

4 cups sourdough bread cubes (1-inch cubes)

2 tbsp olive oil or 1 tbsp melted butter mixed with 1 tbsp olive oil

1 tsp dried Italian seasoning or herbs de Provence

½ tsp garlic powder

Sea salt and freshly ground black pepper to taste

2 tbsp freshly grated Parmesan cheese (optional)

Preheat oven to 350ºF. Line a small rimmed baking sheet with parchment paper.

Arrange bread cubes on baking sheet in a single layer. Drizzle evenly with olive oil and sprinkle with Italian seasoning, garlic powder, salt and pepper. Toss gently using your hands to coat with seasonings. Bake for 15 to 20 minutes, until croutons are golden and crispy. Stir once, halfway through cooking time. Sprinkle with Parmesan at halftime, if using.

Cool completely (they'll get crunchier). Store at room temperature in a resealable plastic bag. Can be frozen.

Makes 4 cups

TOASTY on the outside, SOFT on the inside

Skillet "Roasted" Savory Chickpeas

GF DF V

1 can (19 oz/540 mL) no-salt-added chickpeas, drained and rinsed

1½ tbsp olive oil or avocado oil

½ tsp ground cumin

½ tsp smoked paprika

½ tsp garlic powder

½ tsp dried oregano

¼ tsp sea salt

Pat chickpeas dry with paper towels, removing any loose skins. Heat oil in a 10-inch nonstick skillet over medium heat. Add chickpeas and stir to coat in oil. Sprinkle with spices and mix well. Continue to cook, stir occasionally, until chickpeas are toasty, about 15 minutes. Remove from skillet and let cool. Store leftover chickpeas in an airtight container in the fridge (they will soften).

Makes 2¼ cups

Use as a tasty, protein-packed crouton alternative.

Stovetop Caramelized Pecans

GF

3 tbsp butter

3 tbsp brown sugar (light or dark)

3 tbsp liquid honey

½ tsp cinnamon

¼ tsp sea salt

3 cups pecan halves

Melt butter in a 10-inch nonstick skillet over medium heat. Stir in brown sugar, honey, cinnamon and salt. Cook until mixture is bubbly and sugar has melted. Add pecans and mix well to coat with syrup. Cook and stir for 5 minutes. Be careful not to burn the pecans. Spread hot pecans on parchment paper and cool for 1 hour. Break apart before serving.

Makes 3 cups

Thyme & Black Pepper Parmesan Crisps

GF

4 oz (113 g) freshly grated Parmesan cheese

2 tsp minced fresh thyme

½ tsp freshly ground black pepper

Preheat oven to 375ºF. Line a large baking sheet with parchment paper. In a small bowl, combine Parmesan, thyme and black pepper. Mix well. Mound cheese mixture by the heaping tablespoonful onto baking sheet. Use your fingers to pat down cheese into 2-inch rounds. Don't flatten them completely and leave ½ inch between rounds. Bake for about 7 minutes, or until golden with crisp edges. **Keep an eye on them after 5 minutes**. Remove from oven and cool completely on pan. Once cool, peel crisps off parchment paper. Store in an airtight container.

Makes 14 crisps

Serve with salad,
tomato soup
OR
ENJOY AS A SNACK

Add WOW FACTOR to Mediterranean salads

Lemon & Oregano
Marinated Feta

GF

⅓ cup olive oil

2 tbsp freshly squeezed lemon juice

1 tbsp red wine vinegar

1 tbsp minced shallots

2 tsp minced fresh thyme

2 tsp liquid honey

1 tsp grated lemon zest

½ tsp dried oregano

¼ tsp crushed red pepper flakes

8 oz (227 g) feta cheese (in a block, not crumbled or cubed)

Whisk together all marinade ingredients in a medium bowl. Set aside. Cut feta into ½-inch cubes and add to bowl with marinade. Toss to coat. Cover bowl tightly and marinate for at least 8 hours or overnight, stirring occasionally, for the best flavor. Serve at room temperature. Store for up to 3 days in the fridge. Add wow factor to Mediterranean salads or serve with toothpicks and a side of olives as an appetizer.

Makes 2 cups

A great topper
for
TEX-MEX SALADS,
TACOS OR BURGERS

Mexican Quick-Pickled Onions*

GF DF

1 large red onion

¾ cup freshly squeezed lime juice

¾ cup seasoned rice vinegar

1½ tbsp liquid honey

½ tsp sea salt

¼ tsp cumin seeds

⅛ to ¼ tsp crushed red pepper flakes

Thinly slice onion into ⅛-inch-thick slices. Use a mandoline slicer if you have one (protect your hands!). Pack the onion slices into a 16 oz (500 mL) jar with a lid. In a large measuring cup, whisk together lime juice, vinegar, honey, salt, cumin seeds and crushed red pepper. Pour over onions. Cover and refrigerate for at least 2 hours or “pickle” overnight for the best flavor.

Makes 2 cups

*Not suitable for canning.

The Benefit of the Sprouts:

BIG BANG for your bite *in a tiny package*

Nutrient Powerhouses:

Sprouts are packed with vitamins, minerals and antioxidants.

Flavor Boosters:

Alfalfa or radish sprouts bring a peppery zing, while mung bean or lentil sprouts add a touch of earthiness.

Low-Carb, High Impact:

Sprouts add volume and crunch without the carb overload—a waist-watcher's dream.

Crunchy Wonders:

Sprouts add a fresh, crisp bite to any salad, making every forkful a little more exciting. I love adding crunch to salads!

Healthy Eye Candy:

Their delicate, curly texture (so pretty!) adds a gourmet touch to your homemade salad.

Let's get DRESSED! 

Apple Cider Vinaigrette

GF DF V

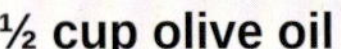

- ½ cup olive oil
- 3 tbsp apple cider vinegar
- 2 tbsp freshly squeezed lemon juice
- 2 tbsp Dijon mustard
- 2 tbsp pure maple syrup
- ¼ tsp each sea salt and freshly ground black pepper

Maple-Balsamic Vinaigrette

GF DF V

- ½ cup olive oil
- ¼ cup balsamic vinegar
- 2 tbsp pure maple syrup
- 1 tbsp freshly squeezed lemon juice
- 1 tbsp Dijon mustard
- 1 tbsp minced shallots (optional)
- ¼ tsp each sea salt and freshly ground black pepper

Parmesan-Italian Dressing

GF

- ½ cup olive oil
- ¼ cup red wine vinegar
- 2 tbsp freshly squeezed lemon juice
- 2 tbsp finely grated Parmesan cheese
- 1 tbsp liquid honey
- 1 tsp minced garlic
- 1 tsp Dijon mustard
- ½ tsp each dried oregano and dried basil
- ¼ tsp each sea salt and freshly ground black pepper

Directions for all dressings:

Whisk together all ingredients in a small bowl or shake well in a mason jar or whirl in a mini blender—the best way to create the silkiest dressings!

Cuz nobody likes a NAKED salad

½ cup olive oil
¼ cup freshly squeezed orange juice
¼ cup white balsamic vinegar
2 tbsp freshly squeezed lemon juice
1 tbsp liquid honey (use pure maple syrup for vegan)
1 tbsp minced shallots
1 tsp Dijon mustard
½ tsp sea salt
¼ tsp freshly ground black pepper

⅓ cup hoisin sauce*
2 tbsp sunflower or peanut oil
2 tbsp dark sesame oil
2 tbsp freshly squeezed lime juice
2 tbsp seasoned rice vinegar
2 tsp grated fresh gingerroot
1 tsp minced garlic
1 tsp grated lime zest†
Pinch crushed red pepper flakes

*For gluten-free, use GF hoisin sauce.

†Try it with orange zest. So good!

⅓ cup tahini (runny)
3 tbsp water (for thinning)
2 tbsp olive oil
2 tbsp freshly squeezed lemon juice
2 tbsp white balsamic vinegar
1 tbsp pure maple syrup
1 tsp reduced-sodium soy sauce*
1 tsp minced garlic (optional)
½ tsp grated lemon zest
¼ tsp sea salt
⅛ tsp freshly ground black pepper

*Use tamari soy sauce for gluten-free.
Drizzle on grain salads or Buddha bowls.

Chick It Out!

Five Flavorful Marinades for Poultry Perfection

Sunny Citrus

- ¼ cup freshly squeezed lime juice
- ¼ cup freshly squeezed orange juice
- 3 tbsp olive oil
- 1 tbsp grainy Dijon mustard
- 1 tbsp liquid honey
- 1 tbsp reduced-sodium soy sauce
- 2 tsp minced garlic
- 2 tsp each grated lime zest and grated orange zest
- Pinch crushed red pepper flakes
- 2 tbsp minced fresh cilantro (optional)

Honey Mustard & Thyme

- ¼ cup liquid honey
- ¼ cup grainy Dijon mustard
- 3 tbsp freshly squeezed lemon juice
- 1 tbsp balsamic vinegar
- 1 tbsp olive oil
- 1 tbsp minced fresh thyme
- 1 tsp grated lemon zest
- ½ tsp each sea salt and freshly ground black pepper

DIRECTIONS: Whisk together all marinade ingredients. Pour over 2 lbs (907 g) chicken thighs or breasts, turn pieces to coat evenly with marinade, cover and refrigerate for 2 hours. Preheat oven to 375ºF. Bake bone-in thighs for 40 to 45 minutes or boneless, skinless breasts for 30 to 35 minutes. Also great on the grill!

Maple, Balsamic & Rosemary

- ¼ cup pure maple syrup
- 3 tbsp freshly squeezed lemon juice
- 2 tbsp grainy Dijon mustard
- 2 tbsp balsamic vinegar
- 1 tbsp minced fresh rosemary
- 2 tsp minced garlic
- 1½ tsp grated lemon zest
- ½ tsp each sea salt and freshly ground black pepper

Greek Souvlaki

- ¼ cup freshly squeezed lemon juice
- 3 tbsp olive oil
- 1½ tbsp red wine vinegar
- 1 tbsp liquid honey
- 2 tsp Dijon mustard
- 2 tsp minced garlic
- 1½ tsp dried oregano
- 1 tsp dried Italian seasoning
- 1 tsp grated lemon zest
- ½ tsp each sea salt and freshly ground black pepper

Asian Hot Honey

- ¼ cup freshly squeezed lime juice
- 3 tbsp hot honey*
- 2 tbsp hoisin sauce
- 1 tbsp reduced-sodium soy sauce
- 2 tbsp minced green onions
- 1 tbsp grated fresh gingerroot
- 1 tbsp minced garlic
- ¼ tsp each ground cumin and chili powder

*Or 3 tbsp regular liquid honey + 1 tbsp Sriracha hot sauce

MAPLE, BALSAMIC & ROSEMARY

GREEK SOUVLAKI

ASIAN HOT HONEY

HONEY MUSTARD & THYME

Lemon & Basil Grilled Shrimp
Shrimp packs
24 G OF PROTEIN
in a 3.5 oz
(100 g) serving

Don't Skimp on the Shrimp!

These lip-smacking marinades will flavor 1½ lbs (680 g) of jumbo, raw shrimp.

Lemon & Basil

GF

⅓ cup minced fresh basil

2 tbsp freshly squeezed lemon juice

1 tbsp each olive oil, melted butter, Dijon mustard and liquid honey

2 tsp each minced garlic, grated fresh gingerroot and grated lemon zest

1 tsp balsamic vinegar

½ tsp sea salt

¼ tsp freshly ground black pepper

Chili, Lime & Cilantro

GF DF

¼ cup freshly squeezed lime juice

3 tbsp olive oil

2 tbsp minced fresh cilantro

1 tbsp liquid honey

2 tsp minced garlic

2 tsp grated lime zest

1 tsp chili powder

1 tsp ground cumin

½ tsp each paprika, sea salt and freshly ground black pepper

DIRECTIONS: Peel and devein shrimp. Whisk together marinade ingredients. Coat shrimp with marinade and refrigerate for 30 minutes to 1 hour max. Thread shrimp onto skewers. Discard marinade. Grill over medium-high heat for 2 to 3 minutes per side or broil on a baking sheet 6 inches from heating element for 2 to 3 minutes per side, until shrimp turns pink and opaque. Tastes great served hot or cold!

Makes 6 skewers

Keep your eyes on the prize! Shrimp cooks very quickly and will turn tough and chewy if you're not paying attention. Promise me you'll stare at them while they're cooking!

How to Make Fish Delish

Two magical marinades for mouthwatering salmon

Lemony Maple & Mustard

3 tbsp freshly squeezed lemon juice
3 tbsp pure maple syrup
3 tbsp grainy Dijon mustard
2 tbsp minced fresh dill
1 tbsp balsamic vinegar
1 tbsp olive oil
2 tsp grated lemon zest
1 tsp minced garlic
¼ tsp each sea salt and freshly ground black pepper

4 boneless skinless salmon fillets, about 6 oz (170 g) each

Whisk together all marinade ingredients and pour over salmon in a lightly oiled glass or ceramic baking dish. Turn salmon to coat both sides with marinade. Cover and refrigerate for 2 hours. Bake (with marinade) at 425ºF for about 15 minutes or until cooked through, depending on thickness of pieces. Makes 4 servings.

Lime & Cilantro

GF DF

¼ cup freshly squeezed lime juice
2 tbsp minced fresh cilantro
1 tbsp reduced-sodium soy sauce*
1 tbsp liquid honey
1 tbsp barbecue sauce
2 tsp Dijon mustard
1 tsp minced garlic
1 tsp grated lime zest
¼ tsp each ground cumin, ground coriander, sea salt and freshly ground black pepper

1½ lbs (680 g) boneless skinless salmon fillets, cut into 1½-inch chunks

*Use tamari soy sauce for gluten-free.

Whisk together all marinade ingredients and pour over salmon cubes in a glass bowl, reserving 2 tbsp marinade for basting. Mix gently to coat salmon with marinade. Cover and refrigerate for 1 hour. Thread salmon cubes onto 10-inch bamboo skewers and place on a nonstick baking sheet. Broil 6 inches from heating element for 3 minutes, turn carefully and continue to cook for another 3 minutes, or until cooked through. Remove from oven and baste with reserved marinade. Makes 6 skewers.

RAISING THE STEAKS:

Mighty meat marinades FOR BEEFING up your salads

Asian Ginger-Hoisin

GF* DF

¼ cup hoisin sauce*

2 tbsp freshly squeezed lime juice

1 tbsp liquid honey

1 tbsp dark sesame oil

1 tbsp reduced-sodium soy sauce*

1 tbsp grated fresh gingerroot

2 tsp minced garlic

2 tsp grated lime zest

Pinch crushed red pepper flakes (optional)

*For gluten-free, use GF hoisin sauce and tamari soy sauce.

Herby Classic

GF DF

2 tbsp balsamic vinegar

2 tbsp grainy Dijon mustard

1 tbsp olive oil

1 tbsp brown sugar

1 tbsp minced fresh rosemary

2 tsp minced garlic

1½ tsp minced fresh thyme

½ tsp each sea salt and freshly ground black pepper

DIRECTIONS: Whisk together all marinade ingredients and pour over 2 lbs (907 g) steaks in a large, heavy-duty, resealable plastic bag. Seal bag and turn several times to coat steaks with marinade. Refrigerate for 2 to 4 hours. Grill steaks on oiled grill racks over medium-high heat for 4 to 5 minutes per side (with lid down), or until your desired degree of doneness. Let rest a couple minutes, then slice and serve. Enjoy!

Pictured using striploin, but also great with tenderloin, sirloin, rib eye and flank steaks.

ACKNOWLEDGMENTS

WRITING AND PUBLISHING A COOKBOOK TAKES A VILLAGE, AND THESE ARE MY VILLAGE PEOPLE.

Janet Podleski, my brilliant, hilarious and ever-supportive sister—though we didn't tackle this book together, your influence is on every page (and probably in a few of my jokes). When I hear voices in my head, one of them is yours, making me laugh. Writing four bestsellers with you was the greatest adventure and, even solo, I still feel like we're in this together. Thank you for being my lifelong co-conspirator and the silliest person I know.

The exceptionally talented people at **REES + STAGER** somehow managed to take my ideas, dreams, words, recipes, food photos and unrealistic expectations of perfection and turn them into the beautiful book you're holding. I truly couldn't have done it without you Brittany, David, Tanya and Janet.

Fina Scroppo, my longtime editor and all-around incredible woman, literally deserves a literary medal for making sense of my nonsensical banter and long-winded, run-on sentences filled with made-up #wrds that don't appear in any reputable sources or dictionaries. Bonus: The Italian in her agreed to be paid for her work in Parmigiano-Reggiano. Grate!

Jackie Mustakas, a beautiful soul and cherished friend, official cheerleader and fellow salad fanatic—you lifted me up, calmed me down and assured me that I wasn't losing my mind—just my avocados to oxidation. Your unwavering support and enthusiasm, in both my work and personal life, mean the world to me.

To my neighbors and always-willing taste-testers (**Mike and Mary Hobin**, **Michael Hecimovich** and **Anne Marie Slegers**), thank you for opening your doors and your mouths to endless bowls of salad. Your *feed*back and encouragement motivated me to keep slicing, dicing and trusting my gut (and yours).

Pete McMenemy, a true friend and official receipt wrangler, thank you for 25+ years of sorting, organizing and calming the chaos. Without you, I'd probably be buried under a mountain of crumpled invoices, wondering where all my money went. I owe you—both figuratively and, most likely, literally. But I can't seem to find the invoice. Sorry!

I'm forever grateful to **Jaime Hayes**, **Kira-Jade Nixon**, **Sophia Reay** and **Jennifer Crawford**, who lent me their glorious garden (Jaime), their fabulous farm (Kira-Jade), their stunning greenhouse (Sophia) and their glue-on eyelashes (Jen) for cookbook photo shoots. (Where have fake eyelashes been all my life? LOL.)

Producing the "Sound Bites" (see page 13) for each recipe required long hours squished into a tiny, padded closet (a.k.a. home recording studio) with **Justin Bott**, a talented, funny, award-winning actor, singer and voiceover artist. Despite the occasional blaring screech from the CO2 monitor, we managed to record 100 episodes in just three days.

INDEX

A

Almonds
- California Quinoa Salad, 28
- Chicken, Mandarin & Avocado Pasta Salad, 104
- Chicken, Strawberry & Avocado Salad, 82
- High-Protein Chicken Salad, 210
- "Rachel Green" Salad, The, 34
- Shaved Brussels Sprouts Salad, 90
- The One with the Ramen Noodles, 182
- Whole Wheat Couscous & Cranberry Salad, 30

Apple Cider Vinaigrette, 62, 262

Apples
- Beet & Apple Salad, 232
- Fresh & Fabulous Fruit Salad, 228
- Galas, Greens & Gorgonzola, 76
- My Wacky Waldorf Salad, 194
- Turkey, Cranberry & Pecan Salad, 224

Arugula
- Blueberry, Nectarine & Arugula Salad, 68
- Roasted Sweet Potato & Brussels Sprout Salad, 242
- Sweet Beet & Balsamic Salad, 220
- Tortellini & Chickpea Salad, 122

Asian Beef Noodle Salad, 98

Asian Chopped Chicken Salad, 56

Asian Cucumber Salad, 244

Asparagus
- Primavera Pesto Pasta Salad, 120

Avocado(s)
- Blueberry, Nectarine & Arugula Salad, 68
- Cannellini, Kale & Avocado Salad, 72
- Chicken, Mandarin & Avocado Pasta Salad, 104
- Chicken, Strawberry & Avocado Salad, 82
- Halloumi, Watermelon & Avocado Salad, 234
- Iconic Cobb Salad, The, 174
- Karmic Kale Pasta Salad, 102
- Pinto Bean, Tomato & Avocado Salad, 156
- Salmon, Avocado & Orange Salad, 88
- Shaved Brussels Sprouts Salad, 90
- Shrimp, Mango & Avocado Salad, 214
- Simple Summery Chickpea Salad, 158
- Steak, Tomato & Avocado Salad, 238
- Tex-Mex Black Bean & Corn Salad, 138
- Tex-Mex Quinoa Salad, 48

B

Bacon
- Broccoli & Bacon Salad, 202
- Caesar Pleaser Salad, 170
- Chicken BLT Pasta Salad, 112
- Iconic Cobb Salad, The, 174
- The Best Baby Spinach Salad, 190
- Warm German Potato Salad, 196
- Warm White Bean & Bacon Salad, 162
- Well-Dressed Wedge Salad, 198

Balsamic dressing, 26, 262

Balsamic glaze, 172, 206

Barley, Beets & Baby Kale Salad, 26

Basil
- Chicken Caprese Pasta Salad, 100
- Chickpea, Tomato & Bocconcini Salad, 134
- Feta Bruschetta Lentil Salad, 160
- Golden Beet Caprese Salad, 206
- Grilled Vegetable Pasta Salad, 114
- Heirloom Tomato Salad, 208
- Panzanella à la Greta, 186
- Roasted Veggie Couscous Salad, 42
- The Beloved Caprese Salad, 172
- Tortellini & Chickpea Salad, 122

BBQ Chopped Chicken Salad, 66

Bean sprouts
- Asian Chopped Chicken Salad, 56

Beans
- about, 130-131
- Black
  - BBQ Chopped Chicken Salad, 66
  - Brown Rice Cowboy Caviar Salad, 18
  - DIY Taco Salad Bar, 240
  - Lentil & Black Bean Salad, 132
  - Tex-Mex Black Bean & Corn Salad, 138
  - Tex-Mex Quinoa Salad, 48
- Black-eyed peas
  - Black-Eyed Pea Salad, 136
- Chickpeas
  - Chickpea & Kidney Bean Salad, 140
  - Chickpea, Tomato & Bocconcini Salad, 134
  - Chopped Cauliflower & Chickpea Salad, 142
  - Easy Peasy Orzo Salad, 126
  - Greek-Style Bulgur Salad, 50
  - Italian Chopped Salad, 178
  - Karmic Kale Pasta Salad, 102
  - Mediterranean Farro Salad, 20
  - Mediterranean Hummus Salad, 212
  - Mediterranean Lentil & Chickpea Salad, 152
  - Mini Cucumber Salad, 230
  - Mom's 4-Bean Salad, 192
  - Moroccan Quinoa Salad, 22
  - Navy Bean & Chickpea Salad, 154
  - "Rachel Green" Salad, The, 34
  - Simple Summery Chickpea Salad, 158
  - Skillet "Roasted" Savory Chickpeas, 251
  - Tortellini & Chickpea Salad, 122
- Cooking from dried, 148-149
- Edamame
  - California Quinoa Salad, 28
  - Crunchy Peanutty Noodle Salad, 106
  - Sunflower Crunch Edamame Salad, 144
  - Vietnamese-Style Jasmine Rice Salad, 46
- Kidney, red
  - Chickpea & Kidney Bean Salad, 140

Mom's 4-Bean Salad, 192
Kidney, white (cannellini)
Cannellini, Kale & Avocado Salad, 72
Tuscan Tuna & White Bean Salad, 150
Warm White Bean & Bacon Salad, 162
Lentils
Copycat Costco Quinoa Salad, 38
Feta Bruschetta Lentil Salad, 160
Lentil & Black Bean Salad, 132
Lentil & Toasted Pine Nut Salad, 146
Mediterranean Lentil & Chickpea Salad, 152
Sunflower Crunch Edamame Salad, 144
Navy
Navy Bean & Chickpea Salad, 154
White Bean Tabbouleh-ish Salad, 164
Pinto
Brown Rice Cowboy Caviar Salad, 18
Pinto Bean, Tomato & Avocado Salad, 156
Beef
Asian Beef Noodle Salad, 98
DIY Taco Salad Bar, 240
Steak marinades
Asian Ginger-Hoisin, 270
Herby Classic, 270
Steak, Tomato & Avocado Salad, 238
Beets
Barley, Beets & Baby Kale Salad, 26
Beet & Apple Salad, 232
Golden Beet Caprese Salad, 206
Sweet Beet & Balsamic Salad, 220
Bell peppers
Green
Brown Rice Cowboy Caviar Salad, 18
Dill-icious Crabmeat Pasta Salad, 108
Lentil & Black Bean Salad, 132
Mom's 4-Bean Salad, 192
My Big Fat Greek Salad, 168
Navy Bean & Chickpea Salad, 154
Orange
Black-Eyed Pea Salad, 136
Tex-Mex Quinoa Salad, 48
Red
Asian Beef Noodle Salad, 98
Asian Chopped Chicken Salad, 56
Brown Rice Cowboy Caviar Salad, 18
California Quinoa Salad, 28
Chicken & Mango Salad, 84
Copycat Costco Quinoa Salad, 38
Crunchy Asian Slaw, 74
Crunchy Peanutty Noodle Salad, 106
Dill-icious Crabmeat Pasta Salad, 108
Everyone's Favorite Creamy Coleslaw, 176
Grilled Vegetable Pasta Salad, 114
High-Protein Chicken Salad, 210
Kale & Quinoa Power Salad, 80
Lentil & Black Bean Salad, 132
Mexican Street Corn Pasta Salad, 118
Moroccan Quinoa Salad, 22
Navy Bean & Chickpea Salad, 154
Primavera Pesto Pasta Salad, 120
Roasted Veggie Couscous Salad, 42
Southwestern Grilled Corn Salad, 216
Spring Roll Salad Bowl, 236
Sunflower Crunch Edamame Salad, 144
Tasty Tuna Noodle Salad, 124
Tex-Mex Black Bean & Corn Salad, 138
Thai Crunch Quinoa Salad, 24
Whole Wheat Couscous & Cranberry Salad, 30
Yellow
Grilled Vegetable Pasta Salad, 114
Italian Chopped Salad, 178
Primavera Pesto Pasta Salad, 120
Roasted Veggie Couscous Salad, 42
Berry Delicious Summer Salad, 58
Black beans
BBQ Chopped Chicken Salad, 66
Brown Rice Cowboy Caviar Salad, 18
DIY Taco Salad Bar, 240
Lentil & Black Bean Salad, 132
Tex-Mex Black Bean & Corn Salad, 138
Tex-Mex Quinoa Salad, 48
Black-eyed peas
Black-Eyed Pea Salad, 136
Blueberries
Berry Delicious Summer Salad, 58
Blueberry, Nectarine & Arugula Salad, 68
Fresh & Fabulous Fruit Salad, 228
Shaved Brussels Sprouts Salad, 90
Blueberry, Nectarine & Arugula Salad, 68
Blue cheese
Galas, Greens & Gorgonzola, 76
Iconic Cobb Salad, The, 174
Well-Dressed Wedge Salad, 198
Bocconcini
Chicken Caprese Pasta Salad, 100
Chickpea, Tomato & Bocconcini Salad, 134
Loaded Italian Pasta Salad, 116
Bottomless Salad for Olive Us, 64
Bread salad (panzanella), 186
Broccoli
Asian Beef Noodle Salad, 98
Broccoli & Bacon Salad, 202
Crunchy Peanutty Noodle Salad, 106
Kale & Quinoa Power Salad, 80
Kale, Brussels Sprouts & Broccoli Slaw, 86
Primavera Pesto Pasta Salad, 120
Brown Rice Cowboy Caviar Salad, 18
Brussels sprouts
Galas, Greens & Gorgonzola, 76
Kale, Brussels Sprouts & Broccoli Slaw, 86
Roasted Sweet Potato & Brussels Sprout Salad, 242
Shaved Brussels Sprouts Salad, 90
Bulgur
Greek-Style Bulgur Salad, 50
Butternut squash
Holiday Grain Salad, 36

C

Cabbage
Green
Everyone's Favorite Creamy Coleslaw, 176
Napa
Asian Chopped Chicken Salad, 56

Crunchy Asian Slaw, 74
Red
Beet & Apple Salad, 232
Crunchy Asian Slaw, 74
My Famous Kaleslaw Salad, 62
Spring Roll Salad Bowl, 236
Sunflower Crunch Edamame Salad, 144
Thai Crunch Quinoa Salad, 24
The One with the Ramen Noodles, 182
Savoy
The One with the Ramen Noodles, 182
Caesar Pleaser Salad, 170
California Quinoa Salad, 28
Cannellini, Kale & Avocado Salad, 72
Caprese salad
Chicken Caprese Pasta Salad, 100
Golden Beet Caprese Salad, 206
The Beloved Caprese Salad, 172
Caramelized Pecans, Stovetop, 253
Carrots
Asian Chopped Chicken Salad, 56
Beet & Apple Salad, 232
Chicken & Mango Salad, 84
Chopped Cauliflower & Chickpea Salad, 142
Crunchy Asian Slaw, 74
Lemony Quinoa Tabbouleh Salad, 44
Moroccan Quinoa Salad, 22
My Famous Kaleslaw Salad, 62
Spring Roll Salad Bowl, 236
Sunflower Crunch Edamame Salad, 144
Thai Crunch Quinoa Salad, 24
The One with the Ramen Noodles, 182
Cauliflower
Chopped Cauliflower & Chickpea Salad, 142
Roasted Cauliflower Salad, 218
Celery
Black-Eyed Pea Salad, 136
Chicken, Mandarin & Avocado Pasta Salad, 104
Chickpea & Kidney Bean Salad, 140
Dill-icious Crabmeat Pasta Salad, 108
Everyone's Favorite Creamy Coleslaw, 176
High-Protein Chicken Salad, 210
Mom's 4-Bean Salad, 192
My Wacky Waldorf Salad, 194
Perfect Picnic Potato Salad, 188
Tasty Tuna Noodle Salad, 124
Turkey, Cranberry & Pecan Salad, 224
Warm German Potato Salad, 196
Cheddar cheese
Broccoli & Bacon Salad, 202
DIY Taco Salad Bar, 240
Cheese. *See Blue, Bocconcini, Cheddar, Cotija, Feta, Halloumi, Mozzarella, Parmesan*
Chicken
Breasts
Asian Chopped Chicken Salad, 56
Chicken & Mango Salad, 84
Chicken BLT Pasta Salad, 112
Chicken Caprese Pasta Salad, 100
Chicken, Mandarin & Avocado Pasta Salad, 104
Chicken, Strawberry & Avocado Salad, 82
Grilled Chicken Souvlaki Salad, 78
Iconic Cobb Salad, The, 174
Marinades
Asian Hot Honey, 265
Greek Souvlaki, 265
Honey Mustard & Thyme, 264
Maple, Balsamic & Rosemary, 265
Sunny Citrus, 264
Rotisserie
High-Protein Chicken Salad, 210
Thighs
BBQ Chopped Chicken Salad, 66
Chickpea & Kidney Bean Salad, 140
Chickpea, Tomato & Bocconcini Salad, 134
Chickpeas
Chickpea & Kidney Bean Salad, 140
Chickpea, Tomato & Bocconcini Salad, 134
Chopped Cauliflower & Chickpea Salad, 142
Easy Peasy Orzo Salad, 126
Greek-Style Bulgur Salad, 50
Italian Chopped Salad, 178
Karmic Kale Pasta Salad, 102
Mediterranean Farro Salad, 20
Mediterranean Hummus Salad, 212
Mediterranean Lentil & Chickpea Salad, 152
Mini Cucumber Salad, 230
Mom's 4-Bean Salad, 192
Moroccan Quinoa Salad, 22
Navy Bean & Chickpea Salad, 154
"Rachel Green" Salad, The, 34
Simple Summery Chickpea Salad, 158
Skillet "Roasted" Savory Chickpeas, 251
Tortellini & Chickpea Salad, 122
Chimichurri
Steak, Tomato & Avocado Salad, 238
Chives
Copycat Costco Quinoa Salad, 38
Well-Dressed Wedge Salad, 198
Chopped Cauliflower & Chickpea Salad, 142
Cilantro
Asian Beef Noodle Salad, 98
Asian Chopped Chicken Salad, 56
BBQ Chopped Chicken Salad, 66
Brown Rice Cowboy Caviar Salad, 18
California Quinoa Salad, 28
Chicken & Mango Salad, 84
Chopped Cauliflower & Chickpea Salad, 142
Crunchy Asian Slaw, 74
Crunchy Peanutty Noodle Salad, 106
DIY Taco Salad Bar, 240
Lentil & Toasted Pine Nut Salad, 146
Mexican Street Corn Pasta Salad, 118
Pinto Bean, Tomato & Avocado Salad, 156
Roasted Cauliflower Salad, 218
Shrimp, Mango & Avocado Salad, 214
Southwestern Grilled Corn Salad, 216
Spring Roll Salad Bowl, 236
Steak, Tomato & Avocado Salad, 238
Sunflower Crunch Edamame Salad, 144
Tex-Mex Black Bean & Corn Salad, 138
Tex-Mex Quinoa Salad, 48
Thai Crunch Quinoa Salad, 24
The One with the Ramen Noodles, 182
Vietnamese-Style Jasmine Rice Salad, 46
Warm White Bean & Bacon Salad, 162

Citrus vinaigrette, 82, 263
Cobb salad, 174
Coconut
California Quinoa Salad, 28
Coleslaw/Slaw
Crunchy Asian Slaw, 74
Everyone's Favorite Creamy Coleslaw, 176
Kale, Brussels Sprouts & Broccoli Slaw, 86
My Famous Kaleslaw Salad, 62
Copycat Costco Quinoa Salad, 38
Corn
BBQ Chopped Chicken Salad, 66
Brown Rice Cowboy Caviar Salad, 18
DIY Taco Salad Bar, 240
Lentil & Black Bean Salad, 132
Mexican Street Corn Pasta Salad, 118
Southwestern Grilled Corn Salad, 216
Tex-Mex Black Bean & Corn Salad, 138
Tex-Mex Quinoa Salad, 48
Cotija cheese
Mexican Street Corn Pasta Salad, 118
Couscous
Roasted Veggie Couscous Salad, 42
Tabbouleh with a Twist, 180
Whole Wheat Couscous & Cranberry Salad, 30
Cowboy Caviar Salad, Brown Rice, 18
Crabmeat
Dill-icious Crabmeat Pasta Salad, 108
Cranberries
Broccoli & Bacon Salad, 202
Kale, Brussels Sprouts & Broccoli Slaw, 86
Lentil & Toasted Pine Nut Salad, 146
My Famous Kaleslaw Salad, 62
"Rachel Green" Salad, The, 34
Turkey, Cranberry & Pecan Salad, 224
Sweet Beet & Balsamic Salad, 220
Whole Wheat Couscous & Cranberry Salad, 30
Croutons, Herb & Garlic Sourdough, 249
Crunchy Asian Slaw, 74
Crunchy Peanutty Noodle Salad, 106
Cucumbers
Asian Beef Noodle Salad, 98
Asian Cucumber Salad, 244
Black-Eyed Pea Salad, 136
Blueberry, Nectarine & Arugula Salad, 68
Chicken, Strawberry & Avocado Salad, 82
Chickpea & Kidney Bean Salad, 140
Copycat Costco Quinoa Salad, 38
Crunchy Peanutty Noodle Salad, 106
Easy Peasy Orzo Salad, 126
Feta Bruschetta Lentil Salad, 160
Greek Penne Pasta Salad, 96
Greek-Style Bulgur Salad, 50
Grilled Chicken Souvlaki Salad, 78
Italian Chopped Salad, 178
Lemony Quinoa Tabbouleh Salad, 44
Lentil & Toasted Pine Nut Salad, 146
Mediterranean Farro Salad, 20
Mediterranean Hummus Salad, 212
Mediterranean Lentil & Chickpea Salad, 152
Mini Cucumber Salad, 230
Moroccan Quinoa Salad, 22
My Big Fat Greek Salad, 168
Panzanella à la Greta, 186
"Rachel Green" Salad, The, 34
Salmon, Avocado & Orange Salad, 88
Shrimp, Mango & Avocado Salad, 214
Simple Summery Chickpea Salad, 158
Spring Roll Salad Bowl, 236
Strawberry & Watermelon Salad, 226
Sunflower Crunch Edamame Salad, 144
Tabbouleh with a Twist, 180
Thai Crunch Quinoa Salad, 24
Tortellini & Chickpea Salad, 122
Tuscan Tuna & White Bean Salad, 150
Vietnamese-Style Jasmine Rice Salad, 46
White Bean Tabbouleh-ish Salad, 164
Whole Wheat Couscous & Cranberry Salad, 30
Currants
California Quinoa Salad, 28
Moroccan Quinoa Salad, 22

D

Dates
Roasted Cauliflower Salad, 218
Dill
Beet & Apple Salad, 232
Chickpea & Kidney Bean Salad, 140
Dill-icious Crabmeat Pasta Salad, 108
Greek-Style Bulgur Salad, 50
Heirloom Tomato Salad, 208
Mediterranean Lentil & Chickpea Salad, 152
Mini Cucumber Salad, 230
Perfect Picnic Potato Salad, 188
Simple Summery Chickpea Salad, 158
Tuscan Tuna & White Bean Salad, 150
Ditali
Mexican Street Corn Pasta Salad, 118
DIY Taco Salad Bar, 240
Dressings
Apple cider vinaigrette, 62, 262
Blue cheese, 198
Caesar, 170
Citrus vinaigrette, 82, 263
Creamy balsamic vinaigrette, 26
Creamy coleslaw, 176
Creamy potato salad, 188
Honey-Dijon vinaigrette, 58
Lemon-Tahini dressing, 60, 263
Lemony Greek-yogurt, for chicken salad, 210
Lemony vinaigrette, 34
Maple-balsamic vinaigrette, 262
Maple-Dijon vinaigrette, 242
Parmesan-Italian, 64, 262
Peanut, 24
Pesto vinaigrette, 120
Ranch, 66
Red wine vinaigrette, 174, 178
Sesame-Ginger, 74, 84, 88, 263
Tahini-balsamic, 40, 102
White balsamic vinaigrette, 72, 90

E

Easy Peasy Orzo Salad, 126
Edamame
California Quinoa Salad, 28
Crunchy Peanutty Noodle Salad, 106
Sunflower Crunch Edamame Salad, 144
Vietnamese-Style Jasmine Rice Salad, 46
Eggs
High-Protein Chicken Salad, 210
Iconic Cobb Salad, The, 174
Perfect Picnic Potato Salad, 188
The Best Baby Spinach Salad, 190
The Notable Niçoise Salad, 200
Everyone's Favorite Creamy Coleslaw, 176

F

Farfalle (bow ties)
Grilled Vegetable Pasta Salad, 114
Farro
Mediterranean Farro Salad, 20
Feta Bruschetta Lentil Salad, 160
Feta cheese
Barley, Beets & Baby Kale Salad, 26
Berry Delicious Summer Salad, 58
Blueberry, Nectarine & Arugula Salad, 68
Easy Peasy Orzo Salad, 126
Feta Bruschetta Lentil Salad, 160
Greek Penne Pasta Salad, 96
Grilled Chicken Souvlaki Salad, 78
Grilled Vegetable Pasta Salad, 114
Heirloom Tomato Salad, 208
Holiday Grain Salad, 36
Lemon & Oregano Marinated Feta, 257
Mediterranean Farro Salad, 20
Mediterranean Lentil & Chickpea Salad, 152
My Big Fat Greek Salad, 168
"Rachel Green" Salad, The, 34
Roasted Sweet Potato & Brussels Sprout Salad, 242
Roasted Veggie Couscous Salad, 42
Shaved Brussels Sprouts Salad, 90
Strawberry & Watermelon Salad, 226
Sweet Beet & Balsamic Salad, 220
Fresh & Fabulous Fruit Salad, 228
Fruit(s). *See specific fruits*
Fusilli
Tasty Tuna Noodle Salad, 124

G

Galas, Greens & Gorgonzola, 76
Gemelli
Karmic Kale Pasta Salad, 102
German Potato Salad, Warm, 196
Goat cheese
Really? *See introduction*, 10
Golden Beet Caprese Salad, 206
Grains. *See also specific grains*
about, 16-17, 32-33
Barley
Barley, Beets & Baby Kale Salad, 26
Bulgur
Greek-Style Bulgur Salad, 50
Couscous (I know, not a grain!)
Roasted Veggie Couscous Salad, 42
Tabbouleh with a Twist, 180
Whole Wheat Couscous & Cranberry Salad, 30
Farro
Mediterranean Farro Salad, 20
Holiday Grain Salad, 36
Quinoa
California Quinoa Salad, 28
Copycat Costco Quinoa Salad, 38
Kale & Quinoa Power Salad, 80
Lemony Quinoa Tabbouleh Salad, 44
Moroccan Quinoa Salad, 22
Tex-Mex Quinoa Salad, 48
Thai Crunch Quinoa Salad, 24
Rice
Brown Rice Cowboy Caviar Salad, 18
"Rachel Green" Salad, The, 34
Roasted Sweet Potato Grain Bowls, 40
Vietnamese-Style Jasmine Rice Salad, 46
Grapes
Fresh & Fabulous Fruit Salad, 228
Greek Penne Pasta Salad, 96
Greek salad, 168
Greek-Style Bulgur Salad, 50
Green beans
Mom's 4-Bean Salad, 192
The Notable Niçoise Salad, 200
Green peppers. *See Bell peppers*
Greens
Arugula
Blueberry, Nectarine & Arugula Salad, 68
Roasted Sweet Potato & Brussels Sprout Salad, 242
Sweet Beet & Balsamic Salad, 220
Tortellini & Chickpea Salad, 122
Cabbage
Green
Everyone's Favorite Creamy Coleslaw, 176
Napa
Asian Chopped Chicken Salad, 56
Crunchy Asian Slaw, 74
Red
Beet & Apple Salad, 232
Crunchy Asian Slaw, 74
My Famous Kaleslaw Salad, 62
Thai Crunch Quinoa Salad, 24
Iceberg
DIY Taco Salad Bar, 240
Italian Chopped Salad, 178
Well-Dressed Wedge Salad, 198
Kale
Baby
Barley, Beets & Baby Kale Salad, 26
Curly
Cannellini, Kale & Avocado Salad, 72
Kale & Quinoa Power Salad, 80
Kale, Brussels Sprouts & Broccoli Slaw, 86
Karmic Kale Pasta Salad, 102
My Famous Kaleslaw Salad, 62
Roasted Sweet Potato Grain Bowls, 40

Mixed Greens/Spring Mix
Berry Delicious Summer Salad, 58
Chicken & Mango Salad, 84
Galas, Greens & Gorgonzola, 76
Salmon, Avocado & Orange Salad, 88
The Notable Niçoise Salad, 200
Radicchio
Italian Chopped Salad, 178
Romaine
Asian Chopped Chicken Salad, 56
BBQ Chopped Chicken Salad, 66
Bottomless Salad for Olive Us, 64
Caesar Pleaser Salad, 170
Grilled Chicken Souvlaki Salad, 78
Grilled Romaine Hearts, 60
Iconic Cobb Salad, The, 174
Spinach
Chicken, Strawberry & Avocado Salad, 82
The Best Baby Spinach Salad, 190
Grilled Chicken Souvlaki Salad, 78
Grilled Corn Salad, Southwestern, 216
Grilled Romaine Hearts, 60
Grilled Vegetable Pasta Salad, 114

H

Halloumi cheese
Halloumi, Watermelon & Avocado Salad, 234
Heirloom Tomato Salad, 208
Hemp hearts
Cannellini, Kale & Avocado Salad, 72
Herb & Garlic Sourdough Croutons, 249
Herbs. *See also Basil, Chives, Cilantro, Dill, Oregano, Mint, Parsley*
about, 223
High-Protein Chicken Salad, 210
Holiday Grain Salad, 36
Hummus Salad, Mediterranean, 212

I

Iconic Cobb Salad, The, 174
Italian Chopped Salad, 178
Italian dressing, 64

J

Jasmine Rice Salad, Vietnamese-Style, 46

K

Kalamata olives
Bottomless Salad for Olive Us, 64
Greek Penne Pasta Salad, 96
Grilled Chicken Souvlaki Salad, 78
Italian Chopped Salad, 178
Loaded Italian Pasta Salad, 116
Mediterranean Hummus Salad, 212
Mediterranean Lentil & Chickpea Salad, 152
My Big Fat Greek Salad, 168
Kale
Baby
Barley, Beets & Baby Kale Salad, 26
Curly
Cannellini, Kale & Avocado Salad, 72
Kale, Brussels Sprouts & Broccoli Slaw, 86
Kale & Quinoa Power Salad, 80
Karmic Kale Pasta Salad, 102
My Famous Kaleslaw Salad, 62
Roasted Sweet Potato Grain Bowls, 40
Tips for using in salads, 70-71
Karmic Kale Pasta Salad, 102
Kidney beans
Red
Chickpea & Kidney Bean Salad, 140
Mom's 4-Bean Salad, 192
White (cannellini)
Cannellini, Kale & Avocado Salad, 72
Tuscan Tuna & White Bean Salad, 150
Warm White Bean & Bacon Salad, 162
Kiwi fruit
Fresh & Fabulous Fruit Salad, 228

L

Lemon & Oregano Marinated Feta, 257
Lemon-Tahini dressing, 60, 263
Lemony Quinoa Tabbouleh Salad, 44
Lemony Vinaigrette, 34
Lentil & Black Bean Salad, 132
Lentil & Toasted Pine Nut Salad, 146
Lentils
Copycat Costco Quinoa Salad, 38
Feta Bruschetta Lentil Salad, 160
Lentil & Black Bean Salad, 132
Lentil & Toasted Pine Nut Salad, 146
Mediterranean Lentil & Chickpea Salad, 152
Sunflower Crunch Edamame Salad, 144
Loaded Italian Pasta Salad, 116

M

Mango(es)
California Quinoa Salad, 28
Chicken & Mango Salad, 84
Fresh & Fabulous Fruit Salad, 228
Shrimp, Mango & Avocado Salad, 214
Spring Roll Salad Bowl, 236
Tex-Mex Black Bean & Corn Salad, 138
Maple-Dijon vinaigrette, 242
Maple-Roasted Pecans, 76
Marinades
Chicken
Asian Hot Honey, 265
Greek Souvlaki, 265
Honey Mustard & Thyme, 264
Maple, Balsamic & Rosemary, 265
Sunny Citrus, 264

Salmon
Lemony Maple & Mustard, 268
Lime & Cilantro, 269
Shrimp
Chili, Lime & Cilantro, 267
Lemon & Basil, 266
Steak
Asian Ginger-Hoisin, 270
Herby Classic, 270
Marinated Feta, Lemon & Oregano, 257
Mediterranean Farro Salad, 20
Mediterranean Hummus Salad, 212
Mediterranean Lentil & Chickpea Salad, 152
Mexican Quick-Pickled Onions, 259
Mexican Street Corn Pasta Salad, 118
Mini Cucumber Salad, 230
Mint
Blueberry, Nectarine & Arugula Salad, 68
Easy Peasy Orzo Salad, 126
Fresh & Fabulous Fruit Salad, 228
Halloumi, Watermelon & Avocado Salad, 234
Holiday Grain Salad, 36
Lemony Quinoa Tabbouleh Salad, 44
Moroccan Quinoa Salad, 22
"Rachel Green" Salad, The, 34
Strawberry & Watermelon Salad, 226
Tabbouleh with a Twist, 180
White Bean Tabbouleh-ish Salad, 164
Mom's 4-Bean Salad, 192
Moroccan Quinoa Salad, 22
Mozzarella cheese, fresh
Chicken Caprese Pasta Salad, 100
Chickpea, Tomato & Bocconcini Salad, 134
Golden Beet Caprese Salad, 206
Loaded Italian Pasta Salad, 116
Panzanella à la Greta, 186
The Beloved Caprese Salad, 172
Mushrooms
Grilled Vegetable Pasta Salad, 114
Roasted Veggie Couscous Salad, 42
The Best Baby Spinach Salad, 190
My Big Fat Greek Salad, 168
My Famous Kaleslaw Salad, 62
My Wacky Waldorf Salad, 194

N

Navy Bean & Chickpea Salad, 154
Nectarine(s)
Blueberry, Nectarine & Arugula Salad, 68
Niçoise salad, 200
Noodles. *See Pasta*
Nuts
Almonds
California Quinoa Salad, 28
Chicken, Mandarin & Avocado Pasta Salad, 104
Chicken, Strawberry & Avocado Salad, 82
High-Protein Chicken Salad, 210
"Rachel Green" Salad, The, 34
The One with the Ramen Noodles, 182
Whole Wheat Couscous & Cranberry Salad, 30
Peanuts
Asian Chopped Chicken Salad, 56
Crunchy Asian Slaw, 74
Crunchy Peanutty Noodle Salad, 106
Spring Roll Salad Bowl, 236
Vietnamese-Style Jasmine Rice Salad, 46
Pecans
Galas, Greens & Gorgonzola, 76
Stovetop Caramelized Pecans, 253
Sweet Beet & Balsamic Salad, 220
Turkey, Cranberry & Pecan Salad, 224
Pine Nuts
Golden Beet Caprese Salad, 206
Lentil & Toasted Pine Nut Salad, 146
Roasted Cauliflower Salad, 218
Pistachios
Barley, Beets & Baby Kale Salad, 26
Walnuts
Berry Delicious Summer Salad, 58
My Wacky Waldorf Salad, 194

O

Olives, Kalamata
Bottomless Salad for Olive Us, 64
Greek Penne Pasta Salad, 96
Grilled Chicken Souvlaki Salad, 78
Italian Chopped Salad, 178
Loaded Italian Pasta Salad, 116
Mediterranean Hummus Salad, 212
Mediterranean Lentil & Chickpea Salad, 152
My Big Fat Greek Salad, 168
Onions
Mexican Quick-Pickled Onions, 259
Orange peppers. *See Bell peppers*
Oranges
Mandarin
Chicken, Mandarin & Avocado Pasta Salad, 104
Fresh & Fabulous Fruit Salad, 228
The Best Baby Spinach Salad, 190
The One with the Ramen Noodles, 182
Salmon, Avocado & Orange Salad, 88
Oregano
Greek Penne Pasta Salad, 96
Lemon & Oregano Marinated Feta, 257
Panzanella à la Greta, 186
Orzo
Easy Peasy Orzo Salad, 126

P

Panko-Parmesan Crumbs, 64
Panzanella à la Greta, 186
Parmesan cheese
Caesar Pleaser Salad, 170
Grilled Romaine Hearts, 60
Italian Chopped Salad, 178
Kale & Quinoa Power Salad, 80
Karmic Kale Pasta Salad, 102
Panko-Parmesan Crumbs, 64
Parmesan-Italian dressing, 64, 262

Primavera Pesto Pasta Salad, 120
Thyme & Black Pepper Parmesan Crisps, 254
Tortellini & Chickpea Salad, 122
Parsley
Beet & Apple Salad, 232
Black-Eyed Pea Salad, 136
Chicken, Mandarin & Avocado Pasta Salad, 104
Chickpea & Kidney Bean Salad, 140
Copycat Costco Quinoa Salad, 38
Greek-Style Bulgur Salad, 50
High-Protein Chicken Salad, 210
Holiday Grain Salad, 36
Lemony Quinoa Tabbouleh Salad, 44
Lentil & Black Bean Salad, 132
Lentil & Toasted Pine Nut Salad, 146
Loaded Italian Pasta Salad, 116
Mediterranean Farro Salad, 20
Mediterranean Lentil & Chickpea Salad, 152
Mom's 4-Bean Salad, 192
My Famous Kaleslaw Salad, 62
My Wacky Waldorf Salad, 194
Navy Bean & Chickpea Salad, 154
Primavera Pesto Pasta Salad, 120
"Rachel Green" Salad, The, 34
Roasted Cauliflower Salad, 218
Steak, Tomato & Avocado Salad, 238
Tabbouleh with a Twist, 180
Tortellini & Chickpea Salad, 122
Turkey, Cranberry & Pecan Salad, 224
Warm German Potato Salad, 196
White Bean Tabbouleh-ish Salad, 164
Whole Wheat Couscous & Cranberry Salad, 30
Pasta
Ditali
Mexican Street Corn Pasta Salad, 118
Farfalle (bow ties)
Grilled Vegetable Pasta Salad, 114
Fusilli
Tasty Tuna Noodle Salad, 124
Gemelli
Karmic Kale Pasta Salad, 102
Orzo
Easy Peasy Orzo Salad, 126
Penne
Greek Penne Pasta Salad, 96
Ramen
The One with the Ramen Noodles, 182
Rotini
Chicken BLT Pasta Salad, 112
Chicken Caprese Pasta Salad, 100
Chicken, Mandarin & Avocado Pasta Salad, 104
Loaded Italian Pasta Salad, 116
My Wacky Waldorf Salad, 194
Primavera Pesto Pasta Salad, 120
Shells
Dill-icious Crabmeat Pasta Salad, 108
Spaghetti
Asian Beef Noodle Salad, 98
Crunchy Peanutty Noodle Salad, 106
Tips for cooking, 110-111
Tortellini
Tortellini & Chickpea Salad, 122
Peanut butter
Crunchy Peanutty Noodle Salad, 106
Thai Crunch Quinoa Salad, 24
Peanut dressing, 24, 56, 106, 236
Peanuts
Asian Chopped Chicken Salad, 56
Crunchy Asian Slaw, 74
Crunchy Peanutty Noodle Salad, 106
Spring Roll Salad Bowl, 236
Vietnamese-Style Jasmine Rice Salad, 46
Pears
Kale & Quinoa Power Salad, 80
Peas
Green
Asian Beef Noodle Salad, 98
Chicken BLT Pasta Salad, 112
Chopped Cauliflower & Chickpea Salad, 142
Easy Peasy Orzo Salad, 126
High-Protein Chicken Salad, 210
Primavera Pesto Pasta Salad, 120
Sugar snap
Crunchy Asian Slaw, 74
Thai Crunch Quinoa Salad, 24
Pecans
Galas, Greens & Gorgonzola, 76
Stovetop Caramelized Pecans, 253
Sweet Beet & Balsamic Salad, 220
Turkey, Cranberry & Pecan Salad, 224
Penne
Greek Penne Pasta Salad, 96
Perfect Picnic Potato Salad, 188
Pesto
Primavera Pesto Pasta Salad, 120
vinaigrette, 120
Pickled Onions, Mexican, 259
Pickles
Perfect Picnic Potato Salad, 188
Tasty Tuna Noodle Salad, 124
Pine Nuts
Golden Beet Caprese Salad, 206
Lentil & Toasted Pine Nut Salad, 146
Roasted Cauliflower Salad, 218
Pinto Bean, Tomato & Avocado Salad, 156
Pistachios
Barley, Beets & Baby Kale Salad, 26
Pomegranate
Beet & Apple Salad, 232
Fresh & Fabulous Fruit Salad, 228
Holiday Grain Salad, 36
Lemony Quinoa Tabbouleh Salad, 44
Roasted Sweet Potato & Brussels Sprout Salad, 242
Poppy seed dressing, 86
Portobello mushrooms
Roasted Veggie Couscous Salad, 42
Potatoes
Red/white
Perfect Picnic Potato Salad, 188
The Notable Niçoise Salad, 200
Warm German Potato Salad, 196
Sweet
Roasted Sweet Potato & Brussels Sprout Salad, 242
Roasted Sweet Potato Grain Bowls, 40
Roasted Veggie Couscous Salad, 42

Primavera Pesto Pasta Salad, 120
Pumpkin seeds
Cannellini, Kale & Avocado Salad, 72
Kale, Brussels Sprouts & Broccoli Slaw, 86
My Famous Kaleslaw Salad, 62
Roasted Sweet Potato & Brussels Sprout Salad, 242

Q

Quick-Pickled Onions, Mexican, 259
Quinoa
California Quinoa Salad, 28
Copycat Costco Quinoa Salad, 38
Kale & Quinoa Power Salad, 80
Lemony Quinoa Tabbouleh Salad, 44
Moroccan Quinoa Salad, 22
Tex-Mex Quinoa Salad, 48
Thai Crunch Quinoa Salad, 24

R

"Rachel Green" Salad, The, 34
Radishes
White Bean Tabbouleh-ish Salad, 164
Raisins
Chopped Cauliflower & Chickpea Salad, 142
Ramen noodle salad, 182
Ranch dressing, 66
Red peppers. *See Bell peppers*
Rice
Brown Rice Cowboy Caviar Salad, 18
"Rachel Green" Salad, The, 34
Roasted Sweet Potato Grain Bowls, 40
Vermicelli noodles
Spring Roll Salad Bowl, 236
Vietnamese-Style Jasmine Rice Salad, 46
Roasted Cauliflower Salad, 218
Roasted red peppers
Loaded Italian Pasta Salad, 116
Roasted Sweet Potato & Brussels Sprout Salad, 242
Roasted Sweet Potato Grain Bowls, 40
Roasted Veggie Couscous Salad, 42
Romaine lettuce
Asian Chopped Chicken Salad, 56
BBQ Chopped Chicken Salad, 66
Bottomless Salad for Olive Us, 64
Chicken BLT Pasta Salad, 112
Grilled Romaine Hearts, 60
Iconic Cobb Salad, The, 174
Spring Roll Salad Bowl, 236
Rotini
Chicken BLT Pasta Salad, 112
Chicken Caprese Pasta Salad, 100
Chicken, Mandarin & Avocado Pasta Salad, 104
Loaded Italian Pasta Salad, 116
My Wacky Waldorf Salad, 194
Primavera Pesto Pasta Salad, 120

S

Salami
Italian Chopped Salad, 178
Loaded Italian Pasta Salad, 116
Salmon, Avocado & Orange Salad, 88
Salmon marinades
Lemony Maple & Mustard, 268
Lime & Cilantro, 269
Sesame-Ginger dressing, 74, 84, 88, 263
Shaved Brussels Sprouts Salad, 90
Shell pasta
Dill-icious Crabmeat Pasta Salad, 108
Shrimp
Marinades
Chili, Lime & Cilantro, 267
Lemon & Basil, 266
Shrimp, Mango & Avocado Salad, 214
Spring Roll Salad Bowl, 236
Simple Summery Chickpea Salad, 158
Skillet "Roasted" Savory Chickpeas, 251
Sourdough Croutons, Herb & Garlic, 249
Southwestern Grilled Corn Salad, 216
Souvlaki salad and marinade, 78
Spaghetti
Asian Beef Noodle Salad, 98
Crunchy Peanutty Noodle Salad, 106
Spinach
Chicken, Strawberry & Avocado Salad, 82
The Best Baby Spinach Salad, 190
Spring Roll Salad Bowl, 236
Sprouts, about, 261
Squash, butternut
Holiday Grain Salad, 36
Steak
Asian Beef Noodle Salad, 98
Marinades
Asian Ginger-Hoisin, 270
Herby Classic, 270
Steak, Tomato & Avocado Salad, 238
Stovetop Caramelized Pecans, 253
Strawberries
Berry Delicious Summer Salad, 58
Chicken, Strawberry & Avocado Salad, 82
Strawberry & Watermelon Salad, 226
Sunflower Crunch Edamame Salad, 144
Sunflower seeds
Broccoli & Bacon Salad, 202
Kale & Quinoa Power Salad, 80
Sunflower Crunch Edamame Salad, 144
Sweet Beet & Balsamic Salad, 220
Sweet Potatoes
Roasted Sweet Potato & Brussels Sprout Salad, 242
Roasted Sweet Potato Grain Bowls, 40
Roasted Veggie Couscous Salad, 42

T

Tabbouleh
Lemony Quinoa Tabbouleh Salad, 44
Tabbouleh with a Twist, 180
White Bean Tabbouleh-ish Salad, 164
Taco Salad Bar, DIY, 240
Taco seasoning, 240

Tahini
Balsamic dressing with, 40, 102
Grilled Romaine Hearts, 60
Lemon-Tahini dressing, 60, 263
Mediterranean Hummus Salad, 212
Roasted Sweet Potato Grain Bowls, 40
Tasty Tuna Noodle Salad, 124
Tex-Mex Black Bean & Corn Salad, 138
Tex-Mex Quinoa Salad, 48
Thai Crunch Quinoa Salad, 24
The Notable Niçoise Salad, 200
The One with the Ramen Noodles, 182
Thyme & Black Pepper Parmesan Crisps, 254
Tomatoes
Cherry/Grape
Chicken BLT Pasta Salad, 112
Chickpea, Tomato & Bocconcini Salad, 134
DIY Taco Salad Bar, 240
Easy Peasy Orzo Salad, 126
Feta Bruschetta Lentil Salad, 160
Greek Penne Pasta Salad, 96
Greek-Style Bulgur Salad, 50
Grilled Chicken Souvlaki Salad, 78
Iconic Cobb Salad, The, 174
Italian Chopped Salad, 178
Karmic Kale Pasta Salad, 102
Lemony Quinoa Tabbouleh Salad, 44
Mediterranean Farro Salad, 20
Mediterranean Hummus Salad, 212
Mediterranean Lentil & Chickpea Salad, 152
Pinto Bean, Tomato & Avocado Salad, 156
Primavera Pesto Pasta Salad, 120
Shrimp, Mango & Avocado Salad, 214
Simple Summery Chickpea Salad, 158
Southwestern Grilled Corn Salad, 216
Tabbouleh with a Twist, 180
Tex-Mex Black Bean & Corn Salad, 138
Tex-Mex Quinoa Salad, 48
The Notable Niçoise Salad, 200
Tortellini & Chickpea Salad, 122
Tuscan Tuna & White Bean Salad, 150
Warm White Bean & Bacon Salad, 162
Well-Dressed Wedge Salad, 198
Heirloom
about, 184
Heirloom Tomato Salad, 208
On-the-vine
My Big Fat Greek Salad, 168
Panzanella à la Greta, 186
Steak, Tomato & Avocado Salad, 238
The Beloved Caprese Salad, 172
Roma (plum)
BBQ Chopped Chicken Salad, 66
Bottomless Salad for Olive Us, 64
White Bean Tabbouleh-ish Salad, 164
Sun-dried
Navy Bean & Chickpea Salad, 154
Tortellini & Chickpea Salad, 122
Tuna
Tasty Tuna Noodle Salad, 124
The Notable Niçoise Salad, 200
Tuscan Tuna & White Bean Salad, 150
Turkey, Cranberry & Pecan Salad, 224
Tzatziki sauce, 50

V

Vegetables. *See individual vegetables*
Vermicelli noodles
Spring Roll Salad Bowl, 236
Vietnamese-Style Jasmine Rice Salad, 46

W

Waldorf pasta salad, 194
Walnuts
Berry Delicious Summer Salad, 58
My Wacky Waldorf Salad, 194
Warm German Potato Salad, 196
Warm White Bean & Bacon Salad, 162
Watermelon
Halloumi, Watermelon & Avocado Salad, 234
Strawberry & Watermelon Salad, 226
Well-Dressed Wedge Salad, 198
White balsamic vinaigrette, 72, 90, 232
White Bean Tabbouleh-ish Salad, 164
Whole Wheat Couscous & Cranberry Salad, 30
Wild Rice
Roasted Sweet Potato Grain Bowls, 40

Y

Yellow peppers. *See Bell peppers*

Z

Zucchini
Grilled Vegetable Pasta Salad, 114
Roasted Veggie Couscous Salad, 42

METRIC CONVERSIONS

Common Kitchen MEASUREMENTS

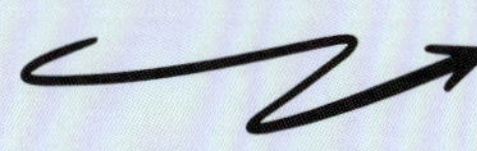

1 pint
2 cups
16 ounces
480 milliliters

1 quart
2 pints
4 cups
32 ounces
950 milliliters

1 gallon
4 quarts
8 pints
16 cups
128 ounces
3.8 liters

1 teaspoon
5 milliliters

1 tablespoon
3 teaspoons
15 milliliters

¼ cup
4 tablespoons
12 teaspoons
2 ounces
60 milliliters

1 cup
8 ounces
250 milliliters

Temperature Conversions

Fahrenheit to Celsius (°F to °C)

500°F = 260°C	350°F = 180°C
475°F = 245°C	325°F = 160°C
450°F = 235°C	300°F = 150°C
425°F = 220°C	275°F = 135°C
400°F = 205°C	250°F = 120°C
375°F = 190°C	225°F = 110°C

Some of life's most flavorful moments can also bring a few tears along the way. And writing this cookbook was no exception. It was a long journey and a true labor of love—one filled with its share of highs, lows and, yes, even some crying. But just like the tears shed while chopping an onion for a cozy, nourishing, homemade meal, it was absolutely worth it.

♥ *Thank you for your support.*